BATTLES OF THE

ELOHIM

THEY WALKED AS MEN

BATTLES OF THE

ELOHIM

THEY WALKED AS MEN

DR. CHRISTIAN HARFOUCHE
DR. ROBIN HARFOUCHE

DESTINY IMAGE® PUBLISHERS, INC.

P.O. Box 310, Shippensburg, PA 17257-0310

"Speaking to the Purposes of God for this Generation and for the Generations to Come."

This book and all other Destiny Image, Revival Press, MercyPlace, Fresh Bread, Destiny Image Fiction, and Treasure House books are available at Christian bookstores and distributors worldwide.

For a U.S. bookstore nearest you, call 1-800-722-6774.

For more information on foreign distributors, call 717-532-3040.

Or reach us on the Internet: www.destinyimage.com

Trade Paper ISBN 13: 978-0-7684-3782-9
Hardcover ISBN 13: 978-0-7684-3783-6
Large Print ISBN13: 978-0-7684-3784-3
Ebook ISBN 13: 978-0-7684-8995-8

For Worldwide Distribution, Printed in the U.S.A.
1 2 3 4 5 6 7 8 9 10 11 / 15 14 13 12 11

TABLE OF CONTENTS

REMOVING THE SHROUD

I heard the booming voice of the Lord say, "There is a spirit that wants to destroy ministry, break covenant, usurp authority, steal from My people, and keep My children trapped with the same patterns that he has used in generations past." What I would see for the next 45 minutes, with open eyes, would be accompanied by the Holy Spirit's clear communication, teaching, instruction, and revelation.

The Spirit of the Lord filled the room and the presence of the Spirit rested strongly upon me. Spiritual things are not easy to put into words, but an atmosphere of somberness and a thick presence would have been experienced by anyone who may have walked into that sacred place. My eyes were filled with tears as the weight of opportunity and responsibility from the Lord seemed to weigh heavy on my heart. As the presence of the Lord continued to move in and increase, it became evident to me that the Lord wanted to disclose some supernatural information.

I saw at a distance the clear, large head of a bull. He faced forty-five degrees away from my gaze. It was evident that a principality of some kind was being revealed. His visage was firm and calculated, and his stillness, coupled with his massive size, made me to know that he has been on assignment for generations. His horns were different from the horns of a bull. They resembled massive horns of a ram and were black and imposing. His color was jet black. He was clearly revealed by the Holy Spirit as a calculated, long-term strategist, who exercises territorial

OPPOSITE
This statue was one of two flanking the entrance to the throne room of King Sargon II, who ruled Assyria over 2700 years ago.

methods of destruction to rule. Many names and characteristics were spoken to us in the ensuing hours, defining, describing, and exposing this age-old spirit.

As I stood there watching this imposing enemy for forty-five minutes or so, an awareness of the power of God and the victory that His children possess filled my mind. I was sure the Lord opened my eyes to uncover the workings of a destructive representative of the dark kingdom, to reveal His answers and His help to man.

I watched the spirit's eyes and his determined focus. He was unaware that I saw him clearly and was not distracted from the direction of his gaze. This was the enemy of humankind—a spirit that instigates the works of the flesh, and presses man to pursue man's own will at the expense of others—the instigator of selfish desires. I was aware that he craves the respect and the obedience of people. This was not an angry, impatient, low-level spirit; but thought himself to be a dignitary of the ruling class that craves and demands the attention and the focus of everything around him. He is the inciter of self-seeking, the fueler of disputes and disagreements, and the motivator of wars. This is a forceful image that motivates the world to seek the strength of the flesh, and the might of one's personal ability; that encourages men to achieve their goals through the agency of misinformation, mischief, misconduct, and by any means necessary. I knew immediately that this force is the obstacle hindering the children of God from receiving the fullness that God has for them, by implementing forceful or natural means intended to distract and deter them.

While uncovering this spirit's method will translate to the blessing of lives; it also translates to a national and international level in our world today. In governments, in economies, in the market place, and in our social life, we see a marked manifestation of those who are driven to seek selfish promotion by means of *pushing* and *shoving*. These are bullying tyrants, that will stop at nothing; willing to lie, manipulate, steal, cheat and control, in order to achieve their personal gain. These negative attributes of achieving personal gain at the expense of others, are directly inspired by the inciter of evil and fanned by this age old spirit.

During the following hours, we were given names of these demonic entities, by the Lord, through the Spirit: Ashteroth (meaning of the two horns, often referred to as "two-horned," and as the "crescent moon" in Easton's Bible Dictionary), the abode of the Rephaim (the greatest giant tribe), Apis (a bull worshipped in Egypt), Bel-Merodach (the chief domestic God of Babylon, who was purported to be the sun god and was in the image of the bull), as well as Adramelech of Assyria, Ashima, Molech and others, as we will relay later.

All truth is parallel; if we know how our enemy has operated in the past, then we can understand how he is operating now. When you know your enemy, you will know not only his weaknesses, but you will also know his strengths. You may think that the dark prince has no strength, but his strength is in his ability to shroud himself in webs of lies and deceit. Sun Tzu in 400 B.C., who wrote the world famous book *The Art of War,*[1] said, *"If you know your enemies and know yourself, you will not be imperiled in a hundred battles."*

Satan's strengths are *in* your compromise. His power *is* your compromise. His ability is contingent upon your disobedience. Contrastingly, his defeat is in your strength and dedication. His lack of ability is in your ability to yield to the Word of God. We are called, not only to be willing, but also to be obedient. This qualifies us for great blessing—to *eat of the good of the land*, as promised in the Word of God. We must be *knowledgeable*. We must be *willing* to know the truth, and we must be *ready* to do something with the truth we know.

There is an invisible war, a battle that is raging; an intensified and dedicated, merciless effort by the spirits of darkness to push the envelope, so to speak, and to press their own agenda upon society. The invisible force that would attempt to stop you is not beyond identification. The spirit of darkness that is on assignment behind the scenes, specializes in confusion, division, and destruction.

When God chose, through His divine providence, to visit us on April 28, 2008, and began to reveal with an open vision for forty-five minutes the dark prince, he wanted me to see with distinct clarity, the form and figure of this age old principality. This knowledge was given from the Lord Himself—names, symptoms, Bible Scriptures, and clear descriptions. God said to us, "*What you see, write it in a book.*" There is a stirring in my spirit regarding a specific timetable for the revealing of the dark prince. *Now* is the time for the world to know their enemy.

As you follow me through this revelation, you will be able to drive miscommunication and division out of your life and relationships. If you are married, the key to continuing in perfect love and agreement will be taught to you from the pages of this book. The dark prince is the covenant destroyer, the author of rebellion, and divorce. He instigates business contracts to be broken and steals your money as well as your promotion. He is the originator of confusion.

The biggest problems we deal with stem from negative bombardment in our thought patterns. These confused thoughts force us to make wrong decisions in our lives. The negative product of these decisions fall on those around us, similar to the domino effect. Oppression, torments, suicidal tendencies, schizophrenia and similar mental illnesses can be directly linked to the dark prince.

It is necessary for us to understand that this spirit is not only against us, individually, but against freedom to worship and prosperous peaceful government. It is important to note that this principality only comes to the forefront whenever he is endeavoring through his strategies to push a one-world agenda. This is the last *one world empire* before his end.

This enormous limestone bull and others like it once overlooked the audience chamber of Darius the great, King of Persia. Sculpted in pairs, atop limestone pillars, these "double bulls" were some of the most elaborate columns in the ancient world, some standing over 95 feet tall.

II

THE ORIGINAL SIN

The Book of Genesis tells the history of Adam and Eve, and how they fell from God's grace. God spoke immediately to Adam, Eve, and the prince of darkness.

> *And LORD God said unto the serpent, Because thou hast done this, thou art cursed above all cattle, and above every beast of the field; upon thy belly shalt thou go, and dust shalt thou eat all the days of thy life: And I will put enmity between thee and the woman, and between thy seed and her seed; it shall bruise thy head, and thou shalt bruise his heel.*[1] As recorded in the book of Genesis and chapter three.[1]

The word *serpent* in the Hebrew is *nachah* which means "snake." The prince of darkness did not transform himself into a snake. He is a fallen angel. The serpent in this account was an actual serpent that was used as his tool. This was a cunning serpent, and there is no doubt that his craftiness was a result of this dark supernatural power. He used this power to cause suspicion to arise in the hearts of Adam and Eve to seduce them to the fall.

OPPOSITE
"Adam and Eve Are Driven out of Eden"
Gustave Dore

The Lord said that he would put *enmity*, which is far greater than hatred, between the seed of the serpent and the *seed of the woman*. God refers to the seed of the woman and not to the seed of man. We will see that this is a mystery even to the powers of darkness, and that this prophecy concerning the coming of the Messiah, the Son of God born of a virgin, is the most essential doctrine of the whole plan of God.

"*For that reason the Lord himself shall give you a sign; Behold, a virgin shall conceive, and bear a son, and shall call his name Immanuel,*" recorded by the prophet Isaiah in the seventh chapter and the fourteenth verse. Immanuel literally means "God with us; as if dwelling in a tent." This Scripture records a very clear prophetic word given by the prophet Isaiah concerning the supernatural conception of the Savior of the world. The fulfillment of this took place when Gabriel the archangel visited the virgin Mary.[2] This visitation is directly linked to the prophetic word originally given in the garden by God. The seed of the woman will come, and in His conquest deal a mortal wound to the dark ruler. The coming Immanuel, the word of God becoming flesh, would bring the presence of God to forever live with humanity. This would be accomplished first through Christ, and then through those who believe in Him through His earthly ministry.

Immanuel is the presence of God upon people, demonstrated fully in the life of Jesus, who was both conceived by, and born of a virgin. Despite myth that infers otherwise, this is the only time in the history of humankind where such a miracle of this kind has taken place. Isaiah clearly spoke of a sign that will be given, that a virgin will conceive and bear a son. The angel Gabriel announced to the virgin Mary that this holy child's name would be called Jesus, and that His kingdom would never end. As the promised deliverer, he would deliver us forever from the dominion of the prince of darkness. This prophetic word Isaiah gave had nothing to do with an immediate fulfillment. It was a messianic word regarding a time when God would fulfill His miracle in the life of His chosen virgin.

Paul told the Colossian church,

> *Beware lest any man spoil you through philosophy and vain deceit, after the tradition of men, after the rudiments of the world, and not after Christ. For in him dwelleth all the fulness of the Godhead bodily* (Colossians 2:8-9).

Paul also states that it pleased God that in all things Christ would have supremacy and complete rule. When the Lord sets in motion a miracle of a predicative nature, God is speaking directly for the benefit of people and in opposition to the strategies of darkness. Biblical Scripture clearly speaks about this dark prince and his attitude regarding God's Word. The Book of James says, "*Thou believest that there is one God; thou doest well: the devils also believe, and tremble*".[3] This is an engaging thought—*the devils also believe, and tremble.*

When the Lord spoke to Isaiah concerning the virgin conceiving, He made it perfectly clear that this was a messianic prophecy. Isaiah goes into further detail showing a man will be born of a woman; consequently, he must also be the seed of the woman promised in Genesis. So both man and woman play a role in salvation. Isaiah says a child will be born. The word translated *Child* in the ninth chapter of Isaiah and verse 6 is the Hebrew word *Yallad*: "something born, a lad, an offspring, a boy, a child, a son, or a young one." We know from the Bible that this is Jesus Christ.

Sturz der rebellischen Engel (Overthrow of the Rebel Angels) Sebastiano Ricci, 1720

Isaiah says that the government shall be upon His shoulders.[4] This is very important because God is prophetically disclosing a governmental order—an empire. This government is the authority, rule and right to be the sovereign of all the earth. This is powerful and will be a subject

One of the two Abu Simbel temples, carved directly into a nubian mountainside during the height of the reign of the Pharaohs, who came into power over 5,000 years ago and ruled until 30 B.C. These lasting monuments, and others like them, were a means for the Pharaohs to intimidate and further impose their religion upon the region.

of discussion throughout this book as we delve into the rise and fall of empires. We will examine the works and activities of the spirits of darkness controlling people through false religion, idolatry and ungodly government. We will furthermore discover the dark spirits behind the visible material world. This will be clearly demonstrated in the primitive empires, beginning with Nimrod and "The Sons of the Earth"; through the Assyrian Empire, Babylonia and the Medio-Persian Empires; and continuing through the Grecian Empire and beyond. The dark ruler's activity was evident in Canaan and the pagan regions round about. It thrived in the Egyptian empire with the spirit's efforts to destroy the coming defender and stop the seed of the woman from coming into the Earth. In the days of Moses, as well as in the days of Jesus Christ, demons have roamed the Earth trying to stop the promise of God and His finished work that will ultimately destroy them. This brings great

significance to the government being upon Christ's shoulder.

A spiritual government which constitutes authority and dominion over devils and over all the material things of this world, would be upon His shoulder; and He in turn, would give His people dominion, according to what He declared to Peter and the Church when He said, "I give you the keys of the kingdom of Heaven. Whatever you allow on earth will be allowed in heaven. Whatever you forbid on Earth is forbidden in heaven."[5] I give you authority, according to the Gospel of Luke, over all the power of the adversary and nothing shall by any means hurt you. Clearly we can see then that the "government upon His shoulder," translates to an opportunity for you and I to govern through the name of Jesus, and to rule through the power of God

Relief of the Persian King Xerxes I among the ruins of his palace at Persepolis. He gained power in 485 B.C. and refused his father's title, instead choosing to be called "King of Kings."

THEY CLAIMED TO BE GOD

According to Isaiah there are five titles given to Messiah that cannot be claimed by any other being legitimately.[6] However, we will find that many pharaohs, monarchs and kings have claimed to be gods; including the pretentious Nimrod, Alexander the Great, and Nebuchadnezzar of Babylonia, who took the name *King of Kings*. Titles were craved and coveted by the dark prince and promised to men who would serve him. These pretenders would ally with him to oppose God's people and to try to destroy the worship of Jehovah from under the sun.

Wonderful is the first of these five names of Messiah, and means "*a miracle, wondrous, wonderful, wonders, or a marvelous thing.*" Jesus is a marvelous thing. He is a miracle. Our allegiance to Him assures the supernatural—a necessary thing in the time that we're living in. We are not ignorant to the defeated powers of darkness that have masqueraded themselves, taken on divine forms, and have been celebrated by superstitious man through images and idols, dominating the majority of our Eastern and Western worlds.

The second title that is Messianic in nature is *Counselor.* The Hebrew word is *"the advisor or consultant; to liberate, to guide, or a counselor."* It is translated this way a minimum of twenty-four times. This name expresses the idea of a supreme counselor—the one who is qualified to give counsel. We know from the Word of God that Christ is Wonderful, Counselor, Mighty God, Everlasting Father, and Prince of Peace. We also know from the Word of God that Jesus said, "I will send you another Comforter" and that when the Holy Ghost is come, He will not speak of Himself but lead us into all truth.[7] We know that He is declared to be our Helper. According to Romans chapter eight, the Holy Spirit will help us in this victory. We see that the precious Holy Spirit is carrying on the counseling ministry and the directing ministry of our Lord and Savior Jesus Christ, as we go forward in His name.

His third title is the *Mighty God.* This title appears to be the most coveted and widespread among false gods. In Hebrew, the word is Gibbor, meaning "powerful, mighty, strong, champion or chief"; "El" or almighty—the strong one. Through our study this title of "El" was unjustly and illegally claimed. Diabolical, devilish spirits led the people in Canaan, in Babylon, in Assyria, in Greece and Rome, to follow and worship idols or rulers claiming the same title that God has allocated to the one and only Lord and Savior, Jesus Christ. He is the Mighty God. He is the Almighty and the conquering God, according to the very definition of the name given to Him. His qualifications as the Word become flesh, His sinless life, and His triumphant act of death and resurrection, gained Him the right through conquest and victory, to be recognized by all of humanity as the Mighty God — the true "El."

In the fourth title, *Everlasting Father,* He is clearly defined as the Father of time—*"In the beginning was the Word and the Word was with God and the Word was God,"* spoken so eloquently through inspired Scripture.[8] The fifth title is the *Prince of Peace* or the *Peaceful Prince.* He will promote and increase His government and His peace among people. We see that God prophesied again through Isaiah to increase revelation and specificity regarding the seed of the woman that will come according to His promise in the book of Genesis. We must also remember that *"the government shall be upon His shoulder."* God reveals through His prophet Isaiah that there is a coming Child, conceived supernaturally, born of supernatural seed, and given to us. He will carry upon Himself the authority to govern. This is the dominion that He will restore to humanity in the middle of a covetous, bullying world that is pushing and shoving, organizing and centralizing, to gain dominion by means of wealth, power and the force of arms. God has appointed sovereignly, before the dawn of time, His King, His Deliverer, His Ruler; and has made (and has made) you and me joint heirs with Christ as we continue to be believers in Him. This is the mystery that none of the princes of this world or powers of darkness knew.

The government shall be upon His shoulder is *Misrah* or empire. It literally means "*authority to rule and the right to be the sovereign over all the Earth.*" When Jesus ascended on high and received of His Father the gift of the Holy Ghost, that was the power for us to step into a kingdom and a government that Jesus released into the Earth through the legal means of victory over all the powers of the dark world. As we step into this spiritual empire, this supernatural government, we step into the authority to rule and reign in life by Christ Jesus.

That is why we take authority over all the fraudulent godlike forms that the dark prince has managed to manifest in the Earth. As we put God first, as we love Him with all of our being, as we keep His Book or His Word in our mouth, doing it day and night, we will prosper in everything that we do. As we love our neighbor as we love ourselves, we're going to learn how to short circuit the power of the devil off the lives (the lives) of families, and off nations, and that is why we will delay the manifestation of an unrighteous end-time empire until we see the greatest harvest the Earth has ever known.

THE RULE OF THE GIANTS

And it came to pass, when men began to multiply on the face of the earth, and daughters were born unto them, That the sons of God saw the daughters of men that they were fair; and they took them wives of all which they chose. And the LORD said, My spirit shall not always strive with man, for that he also is flesh: yet his days shall be an hundred and twenty years. There were giants in the earth in those days; and also after that, when the sons of God came in unto the daughters of men, and they bare children to them, the same became mighty men which were of old, men of renown. [1]

This records the sins of angels. When the sons of men began to multiply on the face of the earth, daughters were born unto the human race. These daughters were recognized to be beautiful and desirable by God's angels. Some angels that lusted after the daughters of people, went to them and took wives from among them as they would choose. The Scripture shows that this is the source of the giants being born into the earth. This sin of the sons of God, the angels marrying the daughters of humankind, caused their sons to take the form of giants in the earth. The Hebrew definition of *Nephelim*, which is plural of *Nephil*, means a "bully, a tyrant, and a *giant.*" It's translated giant here and in the book of Numbers chapter thirteen and verse thirty-three. The Hebrew word is *Gibbor.*

There seems to have been two eruptions of angels marrying earthly

women—one before the flood and one after the flood. When the sons of God married the daughters of men before the flood, giants were born to them; then after the flood there were also giants, born as a result of these fallen angels marrying the daughters of humankind.[2] These giants were recognized to be bullies. They were also called heroes among the antiquities and among some of the writers like Josephus and many others. This explains the legends and folklore of many ancient cultures. We will discover that people were driven by these so called heroes to fall into idolatry and the worship of devils.

It is important to remember that God had spoken prophetically to Adam and Eve declaring that the seed of the woman will come and bring deliverance.[3] It's also important to remember that the first temptation brought to Adam and Eve in the garden was that they "shall be as gods."[4]

Oral tradition was passed on as father and mother shared with their children, that there is a seed of a woman coming to deliver them. Mankind was looking for a divine visitation because of the prophetic word spoken to them by God. Someone was coming to free people from the curse they had fallen into. The ground was hard to till and God was not talking to them the way He used to. Humanity needed supernatural help to get out of the misery that they were living in.

I would like you to see this quote from our father in the faith, Dr. Lester Sumrall from his book, *The Battle of the Ages*: "The original language would read like this: 'The sons of Elohim saw the daughters of Adam, or *Red Earth*, that they were fair, or beautiful, and they took them wives all of which they lustfully chose."[5] There is a line of thinking that states that the sons of God were the line of Seth and the daughters of men were the line of Cain. I know many subscribe to this particular thought; however, it's important to remember that Seth did not have a son until two hundred and thirty years after creation. His son did not have a son until three hundred and twenty-five years after creation and so where would the sons of Seth have come from? They could not have come from Seth. These marriages that took place when men began to multiply had occurred before Seth had sons given in marriage, according to Dake.[6] It is evident from Scripture and certain historic records that the sons of God were angels and the daughters of mankind were human. Therefore the giants were the offspring of the sons of God.

Scriptural records clearly reveal that the sons of God were fallen angels. Jude verses six and seven reads, *"The angels which kept not their first estate, but left their own habitation, He hath reserved in everlasting chains under darkness unto the judgement of the great day."* The spirits mentioned in First Peter chapter three and verse nineteen are fallen angels; as well as in second Peter chapter two, verse four, where it reads: *"For if God spared not the angels that sinned, but cast them down to hell, and delivered them into chains of darkness, to be reserved unto judgment."* In depth study shows that these angels were being judged for this particular sin that they had committed against God; and for producing giants, who were the bullies and tyrants. These same *bullies*, by utilizing their power and ungodly dominion, would be recognized as heroes and men of renown by the same people that they ruled over.

In the Septuagint and Josephus *Antiquities*, along with the Ante-Nicene Fathers, the proof that the sons of God were angels is superabundant. The expression *"sons of God"* is found only five times in the Old Testament; all in which, it is used of *angels*. It is irrefutable that the passages of Job chapter two, and verse one, refer to *angels*. Also, Daniel calls an *angel* the son of God.[7] It is not possible that *sons of God*

OPPOSITE

A stone depiction of Gilgamesh overpowering a lion, from the palace of Sargon II. It stands over 18 feet tall. Gilgamesh was the king of Uruk, referred to in the Bible as Erech, the second city founded by Nimrod in the plain of Shinar, located 20 miles norh west of Ur. In 1852 excavations of the site of Uruk began. Archeologists have since dated the ruins back to near 4000 B.C.. Gilgamesh came to power around 2700 B.C. and was described by his followers as being "Two parts god, one part man."

17

in the book of beginnings would not be angels. Some translations read *"angels of God."* It's very clear in these translations that the angels of God cohabited with the daughters of men. The Torah says, *"The divine beings saw how beautiful the daughters of men were and took wives from among those that pleased them."* The New American Bible calls angels the sons of heaven. The James Moffatt says, *"The angels noticed that the daughters of men were beautiful, and they married them."* An American Translation reads, *"the sons of the gods noticed that the daughters of men were attractive, so they married whom they liked best."*

It's relevant that God had given a prophetic word concerning a coming Redeemer, the seed of the woman, which means supernatural conception. It's not the seed of a man; it is the seed of a woman and implies divine intervention. So humanity was looking for that divine intervention. These angels who fell into sin made a decision and agreed together to choose from the daughters of people, spouses for themselves.

They must have appeared to these women and seduced them to believe they were divine beings that were there to help them bear the offspring that will deliver them from their present dilemmas. Also, Josephus says, "Many angels of God accompanied with women and begat sons that proved unjust and despisers of all that was good because of the confidence they had in their own strength."[8] Flavius Josephus the historian records this as factual truth; of course, he had access to historical records that paralleled the Pentateuch. The first five books of the Bible are called the Pentateuch. These books were given to Moses by God Himself.

Antiquities of Nations says that, "there was a race of the giants who had bodies so large and countenances so entirely different from other men, that they were surprising to the sight and terrible to the hearing."[9] The bones of these men are still shown until this very day, many of which are in private museums, according to Josephus. The book of Josephus reads, "For many angels of God accompanied with women and begat sons that proved unjust, and despisers of all that was good, on account of the confidence they had in their own strength, for the tradition is that these men did what resembled the acts of those whom the Grecians called giants." This notion that fallen angels were the fathers of the old giants[10] was the constant opinion of antiquity. Josephus says further, "The bones of these men are still shown to this very day, unlike to any credible relations of other men."[11]

The Ante-Nicene fathers also referred to angels as falling into "impure love of virgins and were subjected by the flesh. Of these lovers of virgins, therefore, were begotten those who are called of giants."[12] Justin Martyr (A.D. 110-165) remarks, "But the angels transgressed… were captivated by love of women, and begat giants."[13] Methodius (A.D. 260-312) says, "the devil was insolent… as also those angels who were enamored of fleshly charms, and had illicit intercourse with daughters of men."[14] Both testaments of the Bible teach that some of the angels committed sexual sin and lived contrary to nature. Genesis chapter six, verses one through four, gives the history of that sin. It's important to remember that the human race was looking forward to the seed of the woman or the Deliverer.

It is paramount to our study to know the purpose of this dark ruler. He instigated, through the fallen angels, a plan to corrupt the human race and to corrupt the bloodline of pure Adamic stock. This corruption brought forth the giants, titans, and tyrant monarchs. The intention was to halt the prophecy that the offspring of the woman will destroy him. This is the motivation of satan: the corruption of the bloodline, so that he might eliminate Adamic stock from being qualified to give birth to the coming redeemer. The seed that will

The Narmer Palette, carved roughly 5,000 years ago at the very foundation of Egyptian dynastic power, has been called the first historical document in the world. It is thought to depict the unification of upper and lower Egypt into a singular kingdom.

strip him of his authority. It was said to Adam and Eve that the seed of the woman would defeat the dark prince and rescue all humankind. The only way he could stop this was to corrupt the Adamic line, so that he would disqualify them from being able to give birth to the coming Messiah.

The clear revelation that we have of giants in the Scriptures, gives us an understanding of the misinterpretation of Greek mythology. It's very obvious that these giants with their superhuman powers, through adulteration, were misunderstood and eventually regarded as gods. All the nations that came from the union of angels and the daughters of men were giant tribal nations. Some giants had six fingers on each hand and had six toes on each foot. Some of them carried spears weighing from ten to twenty-five pounds according to their stature. Goliath's spearhead weighed twenty-three and one half pounds. The prophet Samuel and Chronicles refers to these giants as being of abnormal size and living in the Earth. The Hebrew word *Nephil* means giant, bully or tyrant. It's very obvious that they were huge, abnormal of size and form, and completely inconsistent with the normal man or woman. The human race in comparison, looked very small.

The Hebrew word *Gibbor*, which we will look at later in titles and names of demigods, angered Jehovah God. It means *"powerful, giant, mighty or strong man."*[15] These words refer to the degree of size and superhuman power or extraordinary strength which was characteristic of every giant people. The *Anakims*, according to the Word of God, were a people great and tall in body. Anak himself was of the giant tribes, and Amman was called a land of giants. Later we will discover some more regarding this name. The *Ammonites* in the Bible were described as *great, many, and tall*. The *Zamzummims* were called giants; or people greatly tall. Bashan is called the land of the giants. A valley of the giants is mentioned in Joshua. The valley of *Rephaim*, the name of another branch of giant race, is often mentioned in Scripture.

In the Book of Genesis it reads, *"And it repented the LORD that He had made man on the earth, and it grieved Him at his heart. And the LORD said, I will destroy man whom I have created from the face of the earth; both man, and beast, and the creeping thing, and the fowls of the air; for it repenteth Me that I have made them."*[16] Also in Genesis it reads, *"The earth also was corrupt before God, and the earth was filled with violence.*

The back of the palette shows King Narmer towering over his shaman and standard bearers as he surveys the remains of his defeated enemies.

On the top left and right of the palette are carvings of the half bull fertility god, Bat, one of the earliest deities worshiped in that part of the world.

And God looked upon the earth, and, behold, it was corrupt; for all flesh had corrupted his way upon the earth."[17]

It's incredibly obvious that the Lord was very repentant, and He was going to act against the attempted plan of the dark prince. The Bible said He sighed or breathed heavily. God expressed sorrow with this heavy sign. He was grieved by the kind of destructive violence that was demonstrated by the human race during the reign of the giants. The Word of God says that the whole earth was corrupt and filled with violence. When you examine these Scriptures hastily you will fail to see the significance of what was taking place. Much of this ancient history is slighted by most people. The word "violence" is the Hebrew word *chamac*, to maltreat. It's a word of injustice, cruelty and oppression. This is obviously the oppression of the giants. We must remember that the efforts to annihilate the Adamic stock were in full force.

God spoke in the book of beginnings about His plan to bring full restoration to the people of the earth. *"And I will put enmity between thee and the woman, and between thy seed and her seed; it shall bruise thy head, and thou shalt bruise His heel.*"[18] This is a direct decree from God that there will come a Redeemer. The offspring of the woman will come. The motivation of fallen angels and of satan, the enemy of God, was to strike first, and intercept what God was promising to humanity.

It is strange and wonderful when we see the sovereign grace of God toward the human race. Genesis states that *"all flesh had been corrupted.*"[19] Josephus follows the history of antiquity and describes the state of mankind, "But for what degree of zeal they had formerly shown for virtue, they now showed by their actions a double decree of wickedness whereby, they made God to be their enemy. For many angels of God accompanied with woman and begat sons that proved unjust and despisers of all that was good on account of their confidence in their own strength."[20]

Notice that Josephus is very strong to describe the wickedness of these giant tribes and the people that were overtaken by them. The sons of angels and women were described as unjust, despisers of all that is good, trusting in their own strength and wickedness. This sheds light on what the Lord described when He said the earth was corrupt and filled with violence.

Again, we must remember that the notion of fallen angels marrying women and producing a giant race was a constant opinion in antiquity. These giants were cruel and profane. They were called bullies, or heroes; and in the King James Bible, they are called men of renown. Also, remember the original definition of some of the giants was the Hebrew word *Gibbor*. It means giant, powerful, mighty, or a strong man. This race hated people and bullied mankind, filling the earth with violence and choosing to rule people by tyranny. These caused chaos and destruction; and strong-armed humanity to sin after their own desires.

JOSEPHUS CONCERNING DAVID & GOLIATH

HOW THE PHILISTINES MADE ANOTHER EXPEDITION AGAINST THE HEBREWS UNDER THE REIGN OF SAUL; AND HOW THEY WERE OVERCOME BY DAVID'S SLAYING GOLIATH IN SINGLE COMBAT.

NOW the Philistines gathered themselves together again not very long time afterward; and having gotten together a great army, they made war against the Israelites; and having seized a place between Shochoh and Azekah, they there pitched their camp. Saul also drew out his army to oppose them; and by pitching his own camp on a certain hill, he forced the Philistines to leave their former camp, and to encamp themselves upon such another hill, over-against that on which Saul's army lay, so that a valley, which was between the two hills on which they lay, divided their camps asunder. Now there came down a man out of the camp of the Philistines, whose name was Goliath, of the city of Gath, a man of vast bulk, for he was of four cubits and a span in tallness, and had about him weapons suitable to the largeness of his body, for he had a breastplate on that weighed five thousand shekels: he had also a helmet and greaves of brass, as large as you would naturally suppose might cover the limbs of so vast a body. His spear was also such as was not

Slings have been used all over the world, since ancient times, for both hunting and war.

carried like a light thing in his right hand, but he carried it as lying on his shoulders. He had also a lance of six hundred shekels; and many followed him to carry his armor. Wherefore this Goliath stood between the two armies, as they were in battle array, and sent out aloud voice, and said to Saul and the Hebrews, "I will free you from fighting and from dangers; for what necessity is there that your army should fall and be afflicted? Give me a man of you that will fight with me, and he that conquers shall have the reward of the conqueror and determine the war; for these shall serve those others to whom the conqueror shall belong; and certainly it is much better, and more prudent, to gain what you desire by the hazard of one man than of all." When he had said this, he retired to his own camp; but the next day he came again, and used the same words, and did not leave off for forty days together, to challenge the enemy in the same words, till Saul and his army were therewith terrified, while they put themselves in array as if they would fight, but did not come to a close battle.

Now while this war between the Hebrews and the Philistines was going on, Saul sent away David to his father Jesse, and contented himself with those three sons of his whom he had sent to his assistance, and to be partners in the dangers of the war: and at first David returned to feed his sheep and his flocks; but after no long time he came to the camp of the Hebrews, as sent by his father, to carry provisions to his brethren, and to know what they were doing. While Goliath came again, and challenged them, and reproached them, that they had no man of valor among them that durst come down to fight him; and as David was talking with his brethren about the business for which his father had sent him, he heard the Philistine reproaching and abusing the army, and had indignation at it, and said to his brethren, "I am ready to fight a single combat with this adversary." Whereupon Eliab, his eldest brother, reproved him, and said that he spoke too rashly and improperly for one of his age, and bid him go to his flocks, and to his father. So he was abashed at his brother's words, and went away, but still he spake to some of the soldiers that he was willing to fight with him that challenged them. And when they had informed Saul what was the resolution of the young man, the king sent for him to come to him: and when the king asked what he had to say, he replied, "O king, be not cast down, nor afraid, for I will depress the insolence of this adversary, and will go down and fight

"David and Goliath" Osmar Schindler

with him, and will bring him under me, as tall and as great as he is, till he shall be sufficiently laughed at, and thy army shall get great glory, when he shall be slain by one that is not yet of man's estate, neither fit for fighting, nor capable of being intrusted with the marshalling an army, or ordering a battle, but by one that looks like a child, and is really no elder in age than a child."

Now Saul wondered at the boldness and alacrity of David, but durst not presume on his ability, by reason of his age; but said he must on that account be too weak to fight with one that was skilled in the art of war. "I undertake this enterprise," said David, "in dependence on God's being with me, for I have had experience already of his assistance; for I once pursued after and caught a lion that assaulted my flocks, and took away a lamb from them; and I snatched the lamb out of the wild beast's mouth, and when he leaped upon me with violence, I took him by the tail, and dashed him against the ground. In the same manner did I avenge myself on a bear also; and let this adversary of ours be esteemed like one of these wild beasts, since he has a long while reproached our army, and blasphemed our God, who yet will reduce him under my power."

However, Saul prayed that the end might be, by God's assistance, not disagreeable to the alacrity and boldness of the child;

and said, "Go thy way to the fight." So he put about him his breastplate, and girded on his sword, and fitted the helmet to his head, and sent him away. But David was burdened with his armor, for he had not been exercised to it, nor had he learned to walk with it; so he said, "Let this armor be thine, O king, who art able to bear it; but give me leave to fight as thy servant, and as I myself desire." Accordingly he laid by the armor, and taking his staff with him, and putting five stones out of the brook into a shepherd's bag, and having a sling in his right hand, he went towards Goliath. But the adversary seeing him come in such a manner, disdained him, and jested upon him, as if he had not such weapons with him as are usual when one man fights against another, but such as are used in driving away and avoiding of dogs; and said, "Dost thou take me not for a man, but a dog?" To which he replied, "No, not for a dog, but for a creature worse than a dog." This provoked Goliath to anger, who thereupon cursed him by the name of God, and threatened to give his flesh to the beasts of the earth, and to the fowls of the air, to be torn in pieces by them. To whom David answered, Thou comest to me with a sword, and with a spear, and with a breastplate; but I have God for my armor in coming against thee, who will destroy thee and all thy army by my hands for I will this day cut off thy head, and cast the other parts of thy body to the dogs, and all men shall learn that God is the protector of the Hebrews, and that our armor and our strength is in his providence; and that without God's assistance, all other warlike preparations and power are useless." So the Philistine being retarded by the weight of his armor, when he attempted to meet David in haste, came on but slowly, as despising him, and depending upon it that he should slay him, who was both unarmed and a child also, without any trouble at all.

But the youth met his antagonist, being accompanied with an invisible assistant, who was no other than God himself. And taking one of the stones that he had out of the brook, and had put into his shepherd's bag, and fitting it to his sling, he slang it against the Philistine. This stone fell upon his forehead, and sank into his brain, insomuch that Goliath was stunned, and fell upon his face. So David ran, and stood upon his adversary as he lay down, and cut off his head with his own sword; for he had no sword himself. And upon the fall of Goliath the Philistines were beaten, and fled; for when they saw their champion prostrate on the ground, they were afraid of the entire issue of their affairs, and resolved not to stay any longer, but committed themselves to an ignominious and indecent flight, and thereby endeavored to save themselves from the dangers they were in. But Saul and the entire army of the Hebrews made a shout, and rushed upon them, and slew a great number of them, and pursued the rest to the borders of Garb, and to the gates of Ekron; so that there were slain of the Philistines thirty thousand, and twice as many wounded. But Saul returned to their camp, and pulled their fortification to pieces, and burnt it; but David carried the head of Goliath into his own tent, but dedicated his sword to God [at the tabernacle].

—Flavius Josephus[21]

THE SONS OF THE EARTH

This history began with Adam and will continue until the flood and afterwards also. Notice that we concluded from our study thus far that the sons of God saw the daughters of men, that they were fair; and the sons of God were the divine ones, or the angels of God. We have shown through many biblical truths that this is fact. We found out that the angels fell, and were being used by the dark prince to bring offspring. These offspring, according to undisputed Antiquities, were used to take over man's territory, and exercise an illegal union to dominate through their bullish, tyrannical natures.

There is a reason why we are going to go into farther depth to address this race of beings that caused God Himself to judge the earth with a flood. These giants were the beginning of the worldwide religion of this dark prince that fell from Heaven. These dark inspired religions, set in motion from the dawn of time, are still in existence today. These are the doctrines of devils Saint Paul speaks of.[1] These religions have oppressed humanity for hundreds and hundreds of generations, and even today, millennia removed, people still do not know the origin of these religions.

It started with the tyrants and titans, giants and angelic offspring; then these offspring of giants carried the traditions of their families. This is the origin of all that is false.

Ignorance is not bliss. Revealing the dark prince will equip humanity with facts to walk, considering God-given knowledge. We must not only be informed, but equipped to discern wickedness in all its shapes and forms. The sons of God saw the daughters of men that they

OPPOSITE
Standing stones can be seen all over the world, and date back to prehistoric times. These enormous upright stones, many weighing tens of thousands of pounds, were erected in a time so far back that we have no records of its peoples, their customs, or the technology and means they used to set up such lasting monuments.

were fair; and took them wives of all which they chose. The Lord said, *"My Spirit shall not always strive with man, for that he also is flesh; yet his days shall be an hundred and twenty years."*[2]

Giants are the titans; these are the Nephilim. The word *Nephil* means *"bully, tyrant, or giant."*[3] Another word for them is *Gibbor* which means "giant" in Job the sixteenth chapter and the fourteenth verse. It is also seen in seventeen other places in the Bible meaning *"giant"* or *"giants."* *Repha,* the Hebrew word, is the root word meaning *Rephaim;*[4] these are the giants that were on the earth in those days.

Where did the giants come from? This answer is clearly evident in Scripture, antiquities, and archeology. These giants came from the angels of God coming to the daughters of men and deceiving them into believing that they are Elohim, members of the "god class." This deception was in contradistinction to the prophecy in the garden given to Adam, Eve, and the dark prince. *The seed of the woman will come to set us free*—this word had been passed down through speech since there was no Bible. So these angels violated their mission. Their job was to be watchers and helpers of people, but they were tempted by what God had created.

The sons of God, or angels, sang together; these are spirits that worshiped and watched God. God created man in His own image and the angels watched. He instructed man and woman in the book of beginnings to have dominion over the entire planet. The sons of God watched God as He created another kind of *son* out of the dust of the planet earth or red earth.

When you trace genealogy back, Adam, who was a new kind of *son*, was capable of love and reproduction. These angelic beings lusted after the beauty of what God had created, and

A 5,400-year-old terracotta fertility idol. Its arms are curled upward to represent the horns of the bull god, the supposed giver of fertility.

coupled with the fall of man, stepped out of obedience to their mission. They went from being *watchers over*, and *givers to*, to becoming *takers from*.

A major stumbling block to most individuals regarding this portion from history is Greek and Roman mythology. I have researched back to bring a bridge of conclusive evidence that will remove the shroud off of this crucial time in our beginning. Greek and Roman mythology distorted all these concepts. We are not criticizing these peoples; but rather, disclosing the doctrines of the dark prince, which have been proliferated from the dawn of time as truth. I have authentic history to reveal ancient secrets which have been mysteriously enveloped by superstition.

The offspring of the dark prince—his abomination—walked as men who lived, died and are buried in the earth. Yes, they were a giant race who intermarried to keep their bloodline pure *giant*. Their religion was directly given to them by their gods, who have been running rampant from then until now, under the guise of false belief, myth and fables. In Syria, Phoenicia, Samaria and in Canaan's land, as well as the Chaldean region of the world, we find these giants. In Spain, in Africa, and in parts of Europe these giant races took possession of the resources of the planet that rightfully belong to humanity.

Two ancient ceramic bull figurines, and a vessel carrying the two horned symbol of a bull from the prehistoric Cucuteni culture. The Cucuteni inhabited eastern Eroupe more than 6,000 years ago and worshiped the celestial bull.

Let's find out a little bit about these giants' form of gods. One of them is *Ashtoreth* which means "two horns." *Ashtoreth* can be found in the Bible in Genesis 14:5; this portion of Scripture explicitly speaks of the *Rephaim*, the greatest of the giant tribes. *Ashtoreth* is also referred to as "crescent moon." We continue our discovery with the worship of *Apis* the bull. The Egyptians believed he was the embodiment of deity. *Bel Merodach* was the chief domestic god of Babylon, who in like manner was the image of a bull.

In the Word of God when you see the word "*El*" or "*Il*" it means strong or mighty. When you see the holy angel Gabriel, that *el* means "strong." When you see Michael, the *el* means strong. The Bible says that the angels excel in strength. So when you see *B-el*... *he* is a fraud.

Bel Merodach is the most ancient deity that you can locate. The dark prince is hiding behind all these images and empowering them. We are living in an age where the dark prince is building an *Invisible Tower of Babel* directly in the center of refined societies. His representatives are being sent to visit politicians, monarchs, dignitaries and ambassadors to move and manipulate massive amounts of wealth; causing an invisible motion of the human race in open rebellion to God. Pushing toward a *one-world* government, with a *one-world* economy and *one-world* religion, that brings a diversity of dark faces into the forefront to rule. This very ancient *Bel Merodach* is found to be synonymous with the Egyptian sun god *Ra*. It is very important to note that the dark prince who was once a holy angel of God knew the titles of Jehovah. He stole these titles and promised them to people.

DOMAIN OF THE TITANS

Titan is the name given to these tribe of giants—sons of the *Nephilim* or *Rephaim*. They occupied, by force of tyranny, Spain, Libya, parts of Africa, and some of the Nordic area. *Titan* was the name given to them as they migrated to dominate geographical regions by force and religion. It is important to understand that this happened before Israel was a nation with the law of Moses.

Enoch *walked* with God. His name means "*initiator*." The original

Tadmor is recorded in I Kings 9:18 and II Chronicles 8:4 as one of the desert cities rebuilt by King Solomon during his reign in Judea.

language of the word translated *walked* means to "*converse with God.*" The earth was being invaded with giant tribes that would eventually be deified as gods. Women thought gods visited them. They became witches or goddesses and gave birth to the titans. Enoch conversed with God; and at this evil time, prophesied the return of the Christ. "*And Enoch also, the seventh from Adam, prophesied of these, saying, Behold, the Lord cometh with ten thousands of his saints, To execute judgment upon all, and to convince all that are ungodly among them of all their ungodly deeds which they have ungodly committed, and of all their hard speeches which ungodly sinners have spoken against him.*"[5] This prophecy is found in the New Testament.

The titans filled the whole earth with violence. The offspring of these giants managed to keep the same religion in every region they dominated. This religion used the same gods but changed their images slightly and their names; thereby localizing this god to every part of the planet. Though these gods had different names, all were *bullish* images; including *Molech*, who was depicted as a man with a bull's head, with his hands outstretched to receive human sacrifice. His arms would be filled with fires up to one hundred feet high. The titans and peoples would beat the drums wildly and throw babies into the flames. The drums were used to drown out the sounds of the screaming child.

Where did Molech and these other gods originate? Paul Pezron, a very respected historian, speaks of *Gomer* in his *Antiquities of Nations*. Gomer was the the eldest son of Jaffet, who was the nephew of Shem.[6]

Flavius Josephus, a respected Jewish historian, has been a great help in our discovery. He is not only well respected, but his historic texts run parallel to the most regarded historians of antiquity. Josephus records in the time of the dispersion after the flood that Gomer, the son of Jaffet, the son of Noah, is the progenitor of the Gomerites, which would become the Galatians, then to be called the *Gauls*.[7]

Far before Alexander the Great and Darius of Persia, these giant tribes ruled the earth. Even farther back in history, before Babylon, Assyria, Medio-Persia, Greece or Rome became empires, these giants ruled and died. They chose to call themselves "Sons of the Earth." This was a time when empires were just domains where princes would rule by force. The titans took the title "prince" and gave it to their toughest, most brutal leader. The titans would set their domain according to physical force and reliance upon the dark knowledge they received directly from fallen angels. They were practitioners of witchcraft and dark arts. Our libraries are full of worthless books. The world's education system is full of errors and myth; people believe in myth but oppose the God of Genesis.

At the time of its assimilation into the Roman Empire, Tadmor was considered one of the wealthiest cities in the near east.

The Carnac stones are an incredibly dense collection of standing stones and other megalithic sites around the French village of Carnac. They are the largest such collection in the world, consisting of over 3,000 individual stones. Its aligned rows of standing stones alone, stretch a combined distance of over two miles.

These Gauls, titans, and barbarian giants were also named "princes of the blood." They intermarried brother to sister or brother to mother, to maintain their bloodline as titan. The fallen angels taught their children to rebel against everything moral or pure. *Immorality* is not a strong enough word to describe these abominations or their religion. Their kings or princes were not only the largest, most powerful, but were the elite educated, and supernaturally inspired in occult practices.

What did they practice? How did they worship? These titans, later deified as gods, terrified the people who would later become Rome. They called themselves, "Children of the Earth," because they wanted to own earth. Some people today place the preservation of the earth above the saving of a human life. Humanity does not belong to the earth; the earth belongs to humanity. This barbarian religion of immorality and witchcraft is dominant today in the earth. It has taken on a polished, intellectual, pro-cultural flavor that appeals to many. Molech is still receiving babies as his worship. People worship *self* as God

Pezron, in the *Antiquities of Nations*, writes that the the ancient fathers—Christians defending the true religion—called Uranus, Saturn and Jupiter, not *gods*, but *titans*—potent princes and mortal men. They knew that these men of war lived and died and were later made gods by their offspring.[8] Ancestral worship is a common practice among many peoples today across the world. These giants or titans were addicted to magic, auguries, satanical delusions, and enchantments. The most feared and reverenced among them performed human sacrifices and were most inclined to profane and diabolical curiosities. Pezron states that the wretched dominion of the Gauls, Gomerites, Gomerians or titans lasted *too long*. The first, second, and third century church fathers found reason to say that giants, tyrants, magicians and enchanters were in the number of the early kings and then afterwards became deified as gods.[9]

The trillithons at Stonehenge each stand over 20 feet tall, and are constructed of three massive stones linked using a complex jointing system. These trillithon stones were transported from a quarry some 25 miles away, most of them weighing in excess of 50,000 pounds.

These giants carried this knowledge from fallen angels in the dawn of history, through their titan religion, into today's contemporary world. It makes perfect sense to conclude that the origin of rebellion comes from the most notorious rebel, and we know that this is satan, that old serpent that fell from his original position in heaven. *Maneus* was the first titan I found, dating back to Genesis.[10] His son was *Acmon*, called *Elion*, by the Phoenicians, according to Sanchoniathon, the esteemed historian of antiquity. Acmon was called Elion or *Almighty*. The son of Acmon was named *Uranus*, literally meaning the "soul of Acmon." Interestingly, *Uranus* was the first to begin the transference of heavenly dark knowledge—fortune telling and soothsaying. He was also called *heaven* and the *soul of Elion*. We will go into greater detail about these titans later in our study.

These are real, idolatrous beings who existed, lived and died, close to the time of Abraham. The very first to be identified is *Maneus*, then *Acmon*, then *Uranus*. The titan princes ruled over territories of Syria and

Phoenicia; and their domain reached far beyond these, even to the Atlantic. The fourth in generation and rulership was named *Saturn*. This titan was the first to crown himself king and wear a robe of royal design. Saturn ruled and died at one hundred and twenty years old, confirmed by the *Chronicles of Alexandria*.[11] Saturn died shortly after Abraham and Sarah gave birth to their son, Isaac.

Saturn's son was *Jupiter*. His reign lasted until his death at one hundred and twenty years old. These titan tribes lived and ruled until as late as five hundred to seven hundred years before Christ. These six generations of titan princes lived and kept their bloodline; ruled by bullish and tyrannical means; served the devil and led armies against humankind. Their tyrannical rule was written in history that parallels our Bible finds. Jupiter is buried on the Island of Crete according to the *Antiquities of Nations*. His tomb was known by location as late as A.D. two hundred and fifty. Jupiter's son was *Mercury*. Mercury went to Egypt on several occasions to learn more soothsaying. He was known to be a false prophet to the gods. He won the favor of Egypt and was given the name *Teutat*. These six generations of titan princes, span from the time of Nabor, the father of Tara, the grandfather of Abraham. We can find that titan princes were in power until Jacob went into Egypt.[12]

Sanchoniathon, a famous historian of antiquity who wrote concerning the Phoenicians, named the person entitled "*Most High*" as Prince Acmon, who died a violent death by wild beast.[13] The Phoenician god Elion is *Baal*. We conclude from our research that Baal and Acmon are the same god in different languages. Pezron confirms that Acmon is named by the Phoenicians as Elion.[14] Baal was a hunter who hunted wild animals for sport just to rip them in pieces.

Titan princes did mighty works and superhuman deeds. They took on themselves the names given in heaven by God. Like most powerful kings of that time they made themselves equal with God. They must have received their information from their fathers, the fallen angels. The works they displayed were supernatural and impossible for man—*godlike*.

People deified these six generations of titan rulers as gods. The first, or oldest, was Maneus, then Acmon, then Uranus, then Saturn, Jupiter, and finally Mercury. We should keep in mind that this transpired before the Grecian and Roman Empires were established; therefore, none of this study includes mythological histories. This study precludes all mythology. You can see how these powerful titans were named gods and later became the thread of fables and myth. Pezron states that the companions of these titans were granted the appellation "*descendants of the gods*."[15] The testimony of Sanchoniathon quoting Eusebius regarding the antiquities of the Phoenicians, calls these companions "*Il*". In the Phoenician tongue it is translated *strong, potent, gods*, or *Elohim*.[16]

The oldest known depiction of Stonehenge, depicting a giant assisting Merlin with its construction.

The peoples who would later become the Grecian Empire consecrated woods and groves to Saturn/Baal in Phrygia and Cappadocia. Pezron cites in his histories that Saturn and Jupiter were warlike and powerful men who ruled nations.[17] Athenagoras, Theophilus of Antioch, Minutieus Felix, Arnobius Lactantius, St. Augustine and others, all state that Saturn, Jupiter, and Mercury were tyrant, titan, giant and warlike people that lived and died a mortal death.[18] Our discovery has opened up an understanding of the present day involvement of this religion in the *push* for all earth to be *one-world*. We will begin to see an undeniable pattern emerge as history repeats itself.

"The Evening of the Deluge"
John Martin

THE MYSTERY OF THE FLOOD

Enoch was one of the very exceptional and unique figures in Bible history. He lived at a time when people did not walk with God. His name meant initiator or forerunner. He was the initiator of a relationship with God when no man had a relationship with Jehovah God. The prophet Enoch was one of three men that were mentioned as godly in the midst of a world that had fallen into degradation and idol worship. Enoch and Noah were the only Antediluvians who walked with God. Able, Enoch and Noah are the only ones referred to in the Bible as being godly during these ancient times.

The Word of God says Enoch walked with God after he had his son Methuselah for three hundred years. Enoch also had other sons and daughters.[1] It is very possible that before Methuselah was born God spoke to His prophet regarding the flood, because his son's name meant, *"when he is dead, it (the deluge) shall come."* Enoch also foretold of the second coming of Christ. He was a very accurate prophet. The Bible says that Enoch *walked* with God. The Hebrew word is *halak*, meaning "to walk up and down and be conversant." This may have been the same type of walk that Adam enjoyed with God in the garden before his fall from grace. We see that through walking with God, Enoch received faith. He was translated, so that he did not see death according to the eleventh chapter of Hebrews. Translating faith must have filled his life as God communicated to him the things that gave him courage; because *"he had this testimony that he pleased God."*[2] He was a man who never saw death. When all of the human race was separated from God, this man maintained three hundred years, believing and pleasing the God that would translate him in the same way as the prophet Elijah. He was a seer—*Enoch was a visionary.*

His son's name, Methuselah, makes it very evident that Enoch heard the Lord. His relationship with God led him to have a revelation regarding a coming supernatural flood that would destroy the wicked. This could be nothing less than supernatural communication from God Himself to the holy man—the prophet that walks with Him. It is obvious and clear that his relationship with God grew as he walked with Him. He drew closer to God each day until he was caught up. Enoch was a very pivotal landmark prophet of that age, displaying the love of God towards the righteous who are willing to *walk* with Him despite persecution.

GOD'S MERCY

It is crucial to remember that *all flesh* had become corrupted and was an

"The Deluge" by Francis Danby. This enormous 15 foot painting depicts the carnage of the flood. In the bottom right corner you can see an angel mourning over the body of his giant offspring.

enemy of God. The effort of the dark prince, his fallen angels, and the religion of the giant tribes had perverted all the people. This threatened the very existence of pure righteous Adamic stock and for that reason threatened the fulfillment of God's promise. The earth was also filled with the violence, the injustice, the bullying, and the tyranny of these giant offspring. They incited man to do evil.

The story of the Ark has been wrapped up by tradition. It is a mystery that must be explained. The neglect and misinterpretation of knowledge regarding the partnership of God with Noah in the actual building of the Ark is incomparable. God chose Noah and his family because they were not polluted with the bloodline of the giant tribes. They were the only pure people left on earth.

The Ark was such a supernatural vessel, masterfully built according to God's specific design to save every species that God will need to repopulate the planet through Noah's righteous family. It is also very noteworthy that up to A.D. 1950, there was no ship as large as the ark.[3] The amazing thing is that in the 1930s, less than 1 percent of the steam ships were as large as the Ark of Noah—possibly the Titanic.[4] Archeological findings further reveal that the Ark had a sewage system unsurpassed by that of any modern city. There were openings for light and ventilations in each storey. It may have been made with *unknown* wood called Gofer. This particular wood is uncertain in origin and cannot be located today.[5] I believe that this may denote God's supernatural involvement in the actual building of the Ark. Divine help must have been offered to Noah to build such an imposing vessel, that would salvage and protect all of God's species. When considering the Ark of Noah, it is very important to remember that a cubit is 25 inches approximately. The Ark was about 625 feet long, 104 feet wide and 62½ feet high. The capacity of the Ark was equivalent in tonnage to more than six hundred freight cars, which would form a train of about five miles long, capable of handling over nine million pounds. The Ark was easily big enough for all it was to hold. The fish and other sea creatures stayed in the sea. Insects were small, as well as snakes and lizards. The average size of most mammals was no larger than a dog. The birds could have easily lodged in the ceilings, or have been hung up in cages. Oxen are allowed 20 square feet on a modern vessel. If this much room was allowed in the Ark for each of the larger mammals, there would have been ample room for all, including food for a year and seventeen days.[6]

The Lord directed Noah to make the Ark with windows on the lower second and third storeys. This word, *Tsohar*, translated *windows*, means an opening for a place of light. This is not the same word translated *window* in Genesis chapter eight and verse six. That word, *challown*, means *one of the windows* in *tsohar* (the place for light for each of the three decks). Tsohar is also translated *noon tide, noon day,* or *noon.* In no Scripture are we told that there was only one small opening in the room where all the foul odors of so many animals, and the refuse was to be removed. We have no indication that God required men and thousands of animals to live in a tight space, without light, ventilation and sanitation for one year and seventeen days. Recent archaeological findings show that this was a very sophisticated vessel that seemed to be far ahead of its time, rivaling some of the very vessels we have on the seas today—all according to Dake.[7] After examining these very clear facts and considering the size of the Ark; the weight of the wood; the way the directions of God specifically designed it to be built; the fact that the wood may be of certain untraceable or unknown origin; along with the sophistication of the sewage systems and ventilations systems that far exceeded the knowledge available at that time, it is not far fetched to believe that divine involvement from angelic beings helped Noah accomplish building the Ark.

We understand that God was grieved in His heart at the wickedness of the human race and that the earth had become full of violence and tyranny. The oppression and the contamination of human beings by the dark powers grieved God. The plan to pollute the bloodline was almost achieved. The supernatural involvement in the actual building of the Ark for the saving of Noah and his household was essential to the plan of God from the book of beginnings. The flood, known by Enoch, was the grace and mercy of Almighty God. *How else was the deliverer going to come?* How else could God save the Adamic stock and preserve a line through which the seed of the woman will come. That is why God judged that He would flood the planet and destroy all rebellious ungodly flesh from the earth.

Noah and his household, and the species delivered from destruction, were used to repopulate the earth. Protecting and perpetuating the Adamic bloodline, and preserving Noah for the purpose of making covenant, would serve as a safeguard and a protection against the sinister work of darkness. The time would come when Christ would redeem humanity from the cunning methods of the dark prince.

The Lord also shut Noah in with his household by closing the door of the Ark Himself. It is also highly possible that He opened it Himself, after the Ark landed on the mountain in Armenia. Flavius Josephus called the Ark's landing the *"the place of descent"*; this is the proper rendering of the Armenian name given to the city built there.[8]

THE NOAHIC COVENANT

The first act of worship that Noah demonstrated toward God was to build an altar and offer an offering—a sacrifice of every fowl and every

A woodcut depicting God helping Noah with the construction of the Ark. By Julius Schnorr von Carolsfeld.

clean beast. Genesis chapter eight verse twenty-one says, *"The Lord smelled the soothing aroma. He said to Himself, 'I will never again curse the ground because of humans, even though from birth their hearts are set on nothing but evil. I will never again kill every living creature as I have just done'"* (GOD'S WORD translation).

Notice that the Lord smelled. This is the Hebrew word *Ruwach* which means *breath, to breath, or to smell.* This should be understood in the sense that God *enjoyed* the smell of that righteous offering. God promised and predicted that because of the obedience and the worship of Noah's offering, He would not curse the ground anymore. God made a covenant with Noah. He had almost destroyed all life in the flood and He promised that He would never do so again by water.

Genesis chapter eight and verse twenty-two says, *"While the earth remaineth, seedtime and harvest, and cold and heat, and summer and winter, and day and night shall not cease."* These are the blessings of God. The covenant He made with Noah is an everlasting covenant—*as long*

Noah receiving the dove with the olive branch. By Andrei Ryabushkin

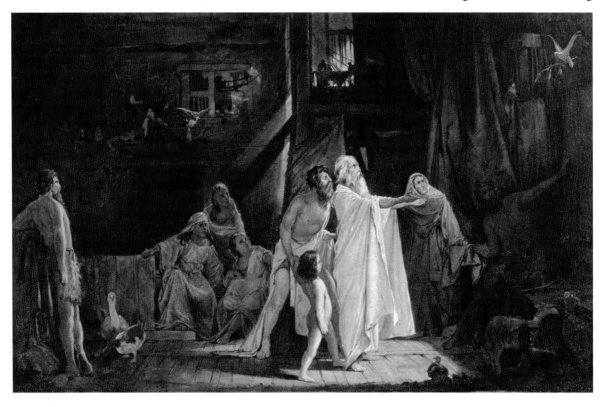

as the earth remains. The kingdom practice of seedtime and harvest will continue to work as long there is cold and heat, summer and winter, day and night. The prosperity and the blessing of the people is predicated upon their willingness to offer to God what He can receive as a sweet smell—an offering that is acceptable to Him.

In the beginning, Abel offered an offering acceptable to God. In turn, Cain revealed himself to be the evil doer who was of the evil one, hating his brother because his own works were evil and his brother's were righteous. Abel, through obedience and worship, offered to God what was pleasing; in this we find the key to the prosperity, the progress, and the experience of the hundredfold that God has in store for His people.

The blessing of God will overtake you—a reality that the enemy hates, fears and loathes with every part of his demonic fiber. This is why he will use every means available, and every kind of deceptive work that is within his arsenal to keep man from worshipping God in spirit and in truth. The dark prince will try to keep people from fulfilling the commandments of God upon which the whole law and the prophets would eventually hinge. Through obedience to these laws, humanity can experience the optimum harvest of prosperity, preservation, protection, divine health, progress, and healing. Love the Lord your God with all your being; have no other gods before Him; and love your neighbor as you love yourself—these are the keys that God has given to His people.[9]

As you look at Genesis eight verse twenty-two again, you will see as far back as the Noahic Covenant that the principle of seedtime and harvest will work for those who please God. For that reason, as long as the earth remains, regardless of the challenges—economic meltdowns, instability in the security of nations, raging angers and wars, the practice of witchcraft, and the antagonism towards Christ—this spiritual law has been set in place. Challenging and turbulent times cannot prevail when we recognize the need to worship God in spirit and in truth.

We must recognize that there is a harvest attached to our seed just as there is cold and heat, summer and winter, and night and day. This will not cease as long as the earth remains. This is the Noahic covenant. We will close this chapter mindful of the blessings of God that are released. It is a Triune blessing.

An image of the flood that shows a giant angel as a symbol for God's protection over Noah and his family.

1st Blessing—**Fruitfulness**, *or Parah* (Hebrew): bear fruit, the power of pro-creation.

2nd Blessing—**Multiplication**, or R*abah* (Hebrew): to increase. It is God's will to increase us in every aspect of our life.

3rd Blessing—**Occupancy**, or M*ala* (Hebrew): to replenish.

OPPOSITE
"The Dove Sent Forth from the Ark."
Gustave Dore

It is entirely possible that the pyramids of Egypt, the giant cities of Bashan, and other huge monuments of construction, will remain an unsolved mystery, unless they are accepted as the result of the labor and the skill of angels. The understanding we have of giants, titans, and tyrants gives us a real picture of what mythology and folklore tried in vain to give.

NIMROD

His name in Hebrew is *Marad* and it means, *to rebel* or *we will rebel*. He lorded over people, hunting and destroying all who would oppose him. He was a psychotic ruler over the minds and the souls of men. This is understood and referenced by Josephus and the writers of the Targums.[1]

Josephus said that Nimrod persuaded men not to attribute their happiness to God but to him. He became a great leader who taught men to centralize, and defied God to send another flood. It is said that Nimrod hunted down wild beasts and taught men to build walls around cities for protection against them.[2]

Genesis chapter ten and verses eight through ten describe this tyrant: "He began to be a mighty one in the earth." "He was a mighty hunter before the Lord." The term *"mighty hunter"* is very fundamental because it could refer to a hunter of animals, or to a hunter of men to enslave them. Nimrod was both a hunter of men and animals. It is our conclusion that he was possessed and driven by an evil demonic nature.

It is logical to believe that Nimrod, who was a tyrant, an oppressive ruler over others in the earth, had a portion with the dark prince. He established the first human kingdom and taught people to build cities. He was the first great propagator of the titan's false religion since the Flood. This was done in open rebellion in the presence of God with all defiance. This is why God would come down to Babel and take action against Nimrod.

The beginning of his kingdom was Babel, and Erech, and Accad,

"The Tower of Babel"
Pieter Bruegel de Oude

and Calneh, in the land of Shinar. Here we have the origin of unification among men. These were not divine institutions as ordained by God to Noah in Genesis chapter nine, but the achievements of lawless tyrants. These rebellious tyrants taught men to revolt against divine laws.

Out of the land of Shinar went forth *Asshur*. He built Nineveh and the city Rehoboth, and Calah. These are great cities constituting the first two empires, Babylon and Assyria.

The book of beginnings chapter eleven and verses one through four reads like this; *"And the whole earth was of one language, and of one speech. And it came to pass, as they journeyed from the east, that they found a plain in the land of Shinar; and they dwelt there. And they said one to another, Go to, let us make brick, and burn them thoroughly. And they had brick for stone, and slime had they for mortar. And they said, Go to, let us build us a city and a tower, whose top may reach unto heaven; and let us make us a name, lest we be scattered abroad upon the face of the whole earth."*

The definition of Nimrod's character and bullish nature, according to the writings of antiquity, strongly imply that this tyrant was the offspring of giants. The Hebrew word *Gibbor*, translated *mighty*, means "a powerful warrior, tyrant, champion, giant or a strong one." It is used of giants who were renowned for wickedness.

At that time in our history the whole earth communicated with one language. Many Bible scholars believe the original language spoken in the earth may have been the Hebrew language from the beginning. We know that God used the Hebrew language to present us with the Old Covenant. Christ speaking to the Apostle Paul on the road to Damascus addressed him in the Hebrew tongue, even though Paul was well acquainted with the Greek language.

Nimrod and his followers settled in the land of Shinar. This means that within one hundred years people had traveled from the mountain of descent in Armenia to east

themselves, Abraham and his servants, slew some as they were in their beds, before they could suspect any harm. Others, who were not yet asleep, but were so drunk that they could not fight, ran away. Abraham pursued after them, till, on the second day, he drove them in a place belonging to Damascus; and thereby demonstrated that victory does not depend on multitude and the number of hands. The speed and courage of soldiers overcame the most numerous bodies of men, while he got the victory over so great an army with no more than three hundred and eighteen of his servants, and three of his friends; but all those that fled returned home ingloriously.[22]

Upon his triumphal return, Abraham had an encounter with Melchizedek, King of Salem, or King of Shalom or Peace. This is the name of the ancient Jerusalem. Melchizedek, according to the teaching of the Word of God, blessed Abraham, and blessed the Most High and credited him with giving this victory to Abraham. Also Melchizedek used the name *"Most High God"* or *"El Elion"* (*El* signifying *"strong"* and

A stone relief showing an Assyrian battering ram attacking a walled city.

"almighty"; "Everlasting God" and "The Mighty One"). Melchizedek received Abraham.[23]

Josephus says that His name signifies, "Righteous King" and such he was, without dispute, insomuch that on this account, he was made the priest of God.[24] However, they afterward called Salem Jerusalem. Now this Melchizedek supplied Abraham's army in a hospitable manner, and gave them provisions in abundance; and as they were feasting, he began to praise and bless God for subduing his enemies under him. And when Abraham gave him the tenth part of his prey—a tithe—he accepted of the gift. This record is of course verified by the writings of Hebrews.[25]

God declared that the Abrahamic covenant would be eternal. The promise to Abraham and his seed is everlasting. This covenant precedes the law of Moses, and this covenant continues to be effective after the conquest of Calvary. This covenant of blessing and multiplication was made by Almighty God to Abraham and his seed.[26]

The Hebrew equals *El Shaddai*. *El* meaning strong one. *Shaddai* means nourisher, strength giver, bountiful supplier of need, satisfier, life giver, and multiplier. This is the covenant made to Abraham and his seed in the book of Galatians, *"And if ye be Christ's, then are ye Abraham's seed, and heirs according to the promise."*[27]

Notice how the prince of darkness from the dawn of time has worked to try to stop the coming seed and the promise; nevertheless, the promise was made by the Strong One. It was made by *El Shaddai*. This meaning bears repeating. *El Shaddai* is the Nourisher, the Strength Giver, the All Bountiful; the Supplier of Need, the Satisfier, the Life-Giver, and the Multiplier.

Because of His ability to make and keep covenant, we who belong to Christ are Abraham's seed and heirs according to the promise, making this eternal covenant of blessing our destiny and our experience.

The Lord also appeared to Abraham's son, Isaac, and made a covenant with him.[28] *Jehovah Elohim* is the God of the individual. I call our God the great individualist. He told Isaac He will multiply his seed as the stars. He said all nations will be blessed in his seed and that he will multiply him, promote him, prosper him, and increase him.

According to the record in Genesis chapter twenty-six, God fulfilled

REVERSE
In this relief you can see the city defenders have deployed a chain in order to immobilize the ram. Two soldiers attempt to detach the chain while being defended by large imposing archers from the rear of the battering ram.

the covenant in Isaac's earthly life. El Shaddai provided multiplication, promotion, prosperity and increase. Isaac sowed in the land during a famine; because of the direction of God, and he reaped a hundred fold. He continued to grow and his enemies envied him.

Isaac's son, the patriarch Jacob was visited by the angels of God. Later he was left alone with just one angel and wrestled until day break. Genesis records this in Scripture, *"And Jacob was left alone; and there wrestled a man with him until the breaking of the day. And when he saw that he prevailed not against him, he touched the hollow of his thigh; and the hollow of Jacob's thigh was out of joint, as he wrestled with him. And he said, Let me go, for the day breaketh. And he said, I will not let thee go, except thou bless me. And he said unto him, What is thy name? And he said, Jacob. And he said, Thy name shall be called no more Jacob, but Israel: for as a prince hast thou power with God and with men, and hast prevailed."* [29]

Jacob was left alone and there appeared to him a man who wrestled with him. Undoubtedly, this was a divine being. The wrestling with which Jacob was involved is called in the Hebrew, *Abaq* meaning "to grapple" or "struggle." It is not the same word used referring to mental struggles. This is physical bodily contact. The Bible again provides us with clarity regarding angels or the Elohim; making it clear in the canon of Scripture that angels could take material form to eat, to fellowship, to commune, to wage war, and to pronounce blessing in the lives of people.[30]

This wrestling and struggling match presented Jacob with an opportunity to prevail with God and to press after the transformation of his nature. His name, Jacob, meant a *supplanter* or *deceiver.* The angel gave him a new name: Israel, meaning a "prince that prevails with God." It is not certain how long this grappling contest took place, but we see that the angel blessed Jacob and changed his name. We can see how the *name* signifies the nature of a man. This is the first recorded reference of the name *Israel.* Jacob was called, "the prince that prevails with God" or "one that has power with God and with man."

Jacob called the name of that place, *Peniel,* meaning in Scripture, *"I have seen God face to face and my life is preserved."*[31] However, one rendition says, "I have seen the face of God and my life is changed."[32]

VIII

THE CHILDREN OF ISRAEL

The Lord had given Abraham direction and a prophetic word regarding his descendants and how they would sojourn in the land of Egypt. The Lord promised that He would bring them out and direct them to the land of Canaan.

Jacob, whose name was changed to Israel, spent his last years in Egypt. He definitely was the most qualified to share with the Egyptians the truth about God since he saw Him face to face. The Bible says that when Jacob met the Pharaoh, he gave him the Lord's blessing.[1]

Joseph, Jacob's son, had already been appointed steward over all of Egypt. He did great and mighty deeds. The children of Israel sojourned in the land of Egypt for four hundred years. The book of Exodus describes this time, beginning with provision and a great multiplication of their tribes. After the tremendous achievements of Joseph, and his stewardship over the grain and all the resources of the land, the children of Israel dwelt peaceably and prosperously in the land of Egypt. They were hardworking and fruitful. The population of Israelites multiplied and increased abundantly. They became mighty, financially prosperous, and the land was filled with them.

OPPOSITE
"Jacob Goeth into Egypt" Gustave Dore

Now there arose up a new sovereign over Egypt who didn't know Joseph. This king was the Assyrian tyrant who overthrew the land of Egypt and made himself Pharaoh. The Hebrew word, *Quwm*, means *stood up; or to stand up in the place of another who is removed*. The founder of this dynasty is believed to be the Assyrian king described in the writings of the prophet Isaiah. He is said to have conquered Egypt; and many sources say that perhaps he was *Ramesses the second*. His son was *Merenptah,* and would be the Pharaoh of Exodus.[2]

The Word of God says that this Assyrian Pharaoh didn't know Joseph.[3] Joseph died approximately one hundred and forty-four years before the nation of Israel left Egypt; this was sixty-four years before Moses was born. This Assyrian Pharaoh started enslaving the tribes of Israel and ordered the murder of all their first born sons. His gods were the bull gods, *Apis, Molech, Bel Merodach,* and the deified *Nimrod*—then known as *Nergal* the mighty hunter. When Moses was born, God protected him and he was adopted by Pharaoh's daughter. It is possible that this Pharoah's son would be the ruler at the time when Moses would come back from the desert to deliver Israel.

The prophet Isaiah states, *"For thus saith the Lord GOD, My people went down aforetime into Egypt to sojourn there; and the Assyrian oppressed them without cause."*[4] This was the Assyrian who conquered Egypt that "knew not Joseph". The Bible goes on to state in the book of Acts, *"But when the time of the promise drew nigh, which God had sworn to Abraham, the people grew and multiplied in Egypt, Till another king arose, which knew not Joseph."*[5]

The book of Acts further says, *"The same* [speaking of the Assyrian Pharaoh] *dealt subtilly with our kindred, and evil entreated our fathers, so that they cast out their young children, to the end they might not live. In which time Moses was born, and was exceeding fair, and nourished up in his father's house three months: And when he was cast out, Pharaoh's daughter took him up, and nourished him for her own son. And Moses was learned in all the wisdom of the Egyptians, and was mighty in words and in deeds."[6]*

It is very significant to note that the most intelligent and best instructed people on earth were taught in the Egyptian Empire. Mercury, the titan, went to Egypt and won the favor of the Egyptians – acquiring the name *Teutat* (found in our study of the *Domains of the Titans.*[7]) The Egyptian learning consisted of the mysteries of religion, arithmetic, geometry, poetry, music, medicine, and hieroglyphics. Moses was instructed in all this knowledge as well as military training. Moses was evidently a general of the Egyptian army and defeated the Ethiopians who had invaded Egypt, according to Josephus whom we will reference.[8]

Josephus records the experience of the children of Israel as thus, "During their occupancy or their sojourning in Egypt, there arose a king that did not know Joseph. Now it happened that the Egyptians grew delicate and lazy, as to pains-taking, and gave themselves up to other pleasures, and in particular to the love of gain. They also became very ill-affected towards the Hebrews, as touched with envy at their prosperity; one of those sacred scribes, who being very sagacious in foretelling future events, told the king, that about this time there would a child be born to the Israelites, who, if he were reared, would bring the Egyptian dominion low, and would raise the Israelites; that he would excel all men in virtue, and obtain a glory that would be remembered through all ages. Which thing was so feared by the king."[9]

The footnote in Josephus mentions that the Targum of Jonathan names the two famous antagonists of Moses, as *Jannes* and *Jambres*.[10]

Grey marble bust of Serapis, a god that is considered the fusion of Apis and Osiris. He is depicted here as having the face of a man on one side and a face of a bull on the other.

He continues, "Nor is it at all unlikely that it might be one of these who foreboded so much misery to the Egyptians, and so much happiness to the Israelites, from the rearing of Moses."[11] The book of Exodus says, *"Now there arose up a new king over Egypt, which knew not Joseph."*[12] It is apparent from the text that until the king rose up that *"knew not Joseph,"* things were prosperous, peaceful, and beneficial for the children of Israel, who simply sojourned in the land of Egypt. This, according to Isaiah's reference was a season when they were not oppressed. They were sojourning. They had peace, prosperity, fruitfulness, and increase until the Assyrian oppressed them without a cause. Some facts to remember: they were fruitful, increased abundantly, multiplied, waxed exceeding mighty, and the land was filled with them. The Assyrian king who had conquered Egypt and became Pharaoh rose up and began to oppress the Hebrews, because of the warnings of the magicians and their soothsaying predictions regarding the birth of a deliverer. A deliverer that would cater to the destruction of the *Egyptian Empire.*

Isis, seen here greeting a Pharaoh, was one of several Egyptian goddesses who were depicted with the horns and sun disc.

An old tradition says that the Pharaoh dreamed of a balance with all Egypt on one scale and a lamb on the other which out-weighed Egypt. The magicians interpreted this to mean that a child was soon to be born to the Hebrews that would destroy the whole of Egypt.[13] It is not far-fetched to see that, again God has placed His promise of deliverance upon a coming seed. The lamb in Pharaoh's dream symbolized the child that would be born to rescue the children of Israel from the tyranny and the dominion of the unjust.

According to both Josephus as well as records of antiquity, this Assyrian king had a dream and several of his soothsayers warned him regarding a lamb, or a ram that would destroy Egypt.[14]

Ironically, the central religion of the Assyrian empire revolved around the same bull god that had spread there through the infamous rebellion of Nimrod and his cohorts. This type of worship was brought into Egypt, entwined with the worship of Apis—the bull of Egypt, and Ra or Amun-Ra—the sun god. It is intriguing to note the fear that gripped this Assyrian Pharaoh's life. It came because of a dream of the victory of a ram that will be used to destroy the power of Egypt and rescue the people of God. This became the primary motivation of this Assyrian Pharaoh to issue an edict for the destruction and the murder of all Hebrew children that would be born. Jehovah protected Moses.

Remember that *Adramelech* was the god of Assyria, related to Molech, identified with Apis (the bull god). These false gods were assimilated into Egypt's worship during the rule of Ramesses II as well as his Assyrian son. The dark prince emerges again on the forefront to destroy the people of God. The Pharaohs spread the worship of the bull during the time of the persecution of the Hebrew children.

As we stated before Nimrod had been deified as a hero hunter in Assyria and identified with the name *Nergal*—the Assyrian deity of

battle. Nimrod who was now named *Nergal,* the Assyrian deity, was molten, and fashioned to resemble a man or a human-headed lion with eagle's wings—called the god of battles. In dynastic times, Pharaoh could be represented as a lion or a bull. During the old kingdom the Egyptians believed that their Pharaoh was a god; they used the same term to describe god and king.

In the book of Exodus we see, *"Therefore they did set over them taskmasters to afflict them with their burdens. And they built for Pharaoh treasure cities, Pithom and Raamses."*[15] The Assyrian Pharaoh, possibly Ramesses II, was moved by these alarming omens and set over the children of Israel taskmasters, with burdens to take advantage of them. He set over them *"sarey missim,"* or chiefs of tribute, to place burdens on them, to set works for them to do, and to exact taxes from them. This Pharaoh collected wealth from them and ruled over them as a superintendent enforcing their public work. Here we see that the wealth of the children of Israel was stolen from them.

This type of spirit covets the wealth, the resources, the labor,

A limestone colossus of Ramesses II from Memphis, the center of Egyptian Apis worship.

and the attention of the people of God. He will do his best to persecute them and strip them of the blessing for fear of the promise of his defeat.

They were made to build store cities of war provisions. They built treasure cities. They built the *city of Ramesses*; built by Ramesses the II and called *the city of the sun*, or *Heliopolis*. This was all done under the pressures of Egyptian superintendents that led them to establish a city for he Egyptian god *Tum*, called *Patumos*. All this was done to give honor to Ramesses II in the capital of Goshen which was also called *On*, and *Heliopolis*,

A relief of Ramesses II being granted his wish for long life by the bull headed god Khnum.

the city of the sun. This is the city where the sun god *Ra* or *Amun-Ra* was worshipped in union and affiliation with associated deities from Assyria, such as Adramelech, Molech, Bel-Merodach, and Nergal.[16] We have seen in our studies how these names were changed and used by the Greeks and other empires, and ascribed to their religion.

Being moved by the influence of this evil spirit, the Pharaoh was mobilized with hatred and a murderous effort to destroy the Hebrews. In Exodus it reads, *"And the king of Egypt spake to the Hebrew midwives, of which the name of the one was Shiphrah, and the name of the other Puah: And he said, When ye do the office of a midwife to the Hebrew women, and see them upon the stools; if it be a son, then ye shall kill him: but if it be a daughter, then she shall live. But the midwives feared God, and did not as the king of Egypt commanded them, but saved the men children alive."*[17]

These midwives knew that this was a sin and that they would incur the death penalty, *"however, they feared God,"* according to Exodus chapter one and verse seventeen. The Hebrew rendering of *God* is

"*Eth ha Elohim*," emphatic for the true God of Israel. They permitted the children to live. It is estimated that there were five hundred to one thousand midwives in Egypt. These midwives were in charge of all the Hebrew births. The midwives probably had to keep records and report to Pharaoh and to his staff.

The historian Josephus is clear that he believed these midwives were Egyptians, and not Hebrews.[18] This seems very probable because how could Pharaoh trust the Israelite midwives to execute so barbarous a command against their own nation. However, whether this is the case or whether the Pharaoh placed Hebrew midwives in charge of overseeing that his orders would be carried out, is in question at this point. The Word of God clearly states the names of the Hebrew midwives. However, Josephus seems to have had much more complete copies of the Pentateuch or other authentic records about the birth of Moses than either our Hebrew or Greek Bibles afford us, which enabled him to be so large in particular about him.

God's divine hand moved in the lives of the midwives. Moses was born and protected by his parents, who put him in a cradle or basket and placed him in the river. Josephus records this account consistently with the Scripture of the Bible. He states in his histories, "When those that were sent on this errand came to *Hur*, Thermuthis the king's daughter, fell greatly in love with the baby on account of its largeness and beauty for God had taken such great care in the formation of Moses, that he caused him to be thought worthy of bringing up, and providing for, by all those that had taken the most fatal resolutions, on account of the dread of his nativity, for the destruction of the rest of the Hebrew nation."[19]

Thermuthis adopted Moses and chose to raise him as her own child. The book of Acts says, *"In which time Moses was born, and was exceeding fair, and nourished up in his father's house three months."*[20] It is recorded that one day the king's daughter, Thermuthis, brought Moses to her father and she presented him to her father as her adopted child. She had no heir and petitioned her father that he would accept him as the potential heir of his kingdom.[21]

The Assyrian Pharaoh, Ramesses II, is purported to have taken him from Thermuthis and hugged him close to his breast, according

The obelisk at the Luxor Temple in Egypt. Errected over 3,000 years ago, this 75 foot high granite column weighs over 550,000 pounds. Its surface is covered in hieroglyphics exalting the reign of Ramesses II.

to Josephus.[22] When the sacred scribe saw this, the very person who foretold that his nativity would bring the dominion of that kingdom low, he made a violent attempt to kill him, and cried out in a frightful manner; he said, "This, O king! this child is he of whom God foretold, that if we kill him we shall be in no danger."[23] We know from our study that the soothsayers, the magicians, the Egyptian's sacred scribes, the dream of the Assyrian Pharaoh were all attributed to their false gods. The dark prince was the power influencing all these men. He remained hidden behind different specific images.

The Bible is clear in teaching that Moses was learned in all the wisdom and the knowledge of the Egyptians.[24] It is well established that Moses served as general of the army of Egypt and was possibly in line to be heir of the throne. This history of Moses that led the army of Egypt in victory over the Ethiopians is cited by Irenaeus as well as Josephus.[25] Josephus records that when Moses was nourished in the king's palace, he was appointed general of the army against the Ethiopians.[26]

These historical records unequivocally correlate with our Bible account that Moses was taught in all the knowledge of the Egyptians and he was mighty in deed. This explains how the children of Israel managed to use military actions in their conflicts against unfriendly tribes during their sojourning in the wilderness.

The Word of God clearly states, through the writings and preaching of Stephen, that Pharaoh's daughter took Moses and nourished him for her own, and that Moses was learned in all the wisdom of the Egyptians.[27] He was mighty in words and in deeds. He was a *great* leader. He was a *qualified* leader.

Moses led the Egyptian military in one of the most important wars they ever had. He defeated the Ethiopians, found favor with the Ethiopian princess and married her. He was a warrior. He was full of wisdom and groomed to be a *Prince of Egypt*. Moses knew their ideologies, the mysticism and Egyptian religion.

We know that Moses would eventually renounce his sonship to Thermuthis, and possibly the even greater opportunity to be Pharaoh of all Egypt. Moses chose God. He counted the riches of Christ greater than the treasures of Egypt. Moses was an extraordinary gentleman.

The Bible calls him a meek man. Moses forsook all of Egypt to fulfill his purpose.

As Moses inspected the slavery of his brethren, he was angry at their treatment and intervened to help, and skillfully slew an Egyptian superintendent. Notice, the next day he was out among the Hebrews and saw two men arguing. Moses tried to intervene again. He inquired

of the men why they were hitting each other. The Hebrews replied with disdain, "Who made you a judge over us?"[28] We must understand that to the Hebrews, Moses was a *Prince of Egypt*. He was their enemy and taskmaster—not their deliverer.

The Bible says the men asked, *"Intendest thou to kill me, as thou has killed the Egyptian?"*[29] Within one day what Moses had done had spread throughout the Hebrew nation. He was an Egyptian general, in line for the throne, a warrior, Pharaoh's son, and he killed one of his own soldiers—*this was news.*

Pharaoh heard about it and wanted to slay Moses. This Moses was attempting to walk in his call. He was trying to unite his people;

This painting shows a Pharaoh destroying his enemies on the field of battle. This type of image was common in ancient Egypt, often shown with the enemies substituted with the Pharaoh's latest conquest.

Mereneptah, the son of Ramesses II. He is shown here wearing the horns and sun disc, signifying his divine rule.

however, by slaying an Egyptian soldier he faced the death penalty. He fled into the wilderness.

Dr. Lester Sumrall told me that Moses had three phases of his life and call. The first was forty years in Egypt; Sumrall said that this signified his *"flesh phase."* The second was in the desert, and that signified the *"soul."* The last or third phase was when God called him from the burning bush to enter into his ministry, and that signified the *"Spirit."*

In the process of time, the Assyrian Pharaoh died and the children of Israel cried out to God for help. Merenptah was now sovereign and increased the persecution of the Hebrews.

Moses kept the flock of Jethro, a priest of Midian, and married Jethro's daughter Zipporah.[30] This *Prince of Egypt* became a shepherd of sheep. It seems as if Moses didn't care anymore. He was rejected by the children of Israel. Josephus says that Moses pastured on Mount Horeb.[31] This is the highest of all the mountains nearby and the very best for pasturage. The herbage there was the choicest quality. It had not been fed on because the other sheep herders were afraid of that mountain. They would not dare climb it because it was a well known fact that God dwelt there.

Moses was not afraid of God and he took that prosperous place as his own. After forty-years of being in the desert the Lord appeared as recorded in Exodus, *"And the angel of the Lord appeared unto him in a flame of fire out of the midst of a bush: and he looked, and, behold the bush burned with fire, and the bush was not consumed."*[32] Josephus writes about Moses and the burning bush: "For a fire fed upon a thorn bush, yet did the green leaves and the flowers continue untouched, and the fire did not at all consume the fruit branches, although the flame was great and fierce."[33] This is why Moses turned aside to see the bush: because it was not consumed. It seems that the record of Josephus, "of the fierceness of the flame" is accurate. The angel of the Lord spoke out of the burning bush to Moses.

The angels of God are exceedingly imposing and very powerful to look at, according to the Books of Hebrew which reads, *"And of the angels he saith, Who maketh his angels spirits, and his ministers a flame of fire."*[34] The fire that covered the angel was equivalent to His size and therefore would have been a fierce sight to Moses. He was accustomed to the worship of Egypt and especially, of *Molech,* but this miraculous demonstration of Jehovah was entirely different.

Exodus records as follows, *"And he said, Draw not nigh hither: put off thy shoes from off thy feet, for the place whereon thou standest is holy ground. Moreover he said, I am the God of thy father, the God of Abraham, the God of Isaac, and the God of Jacob. And Moses hid his face; for he was afraid to look upon God. And the Lord said, I have surely seen the affliction of my people which are in Egypt, and have heard their cry by reason of their taskmasters; for I know their sorrows."*[35]

The historian Josephus writes concerning this event, "Now this is

A sphinx bearing the name of Mereneptah. It was common for sculptures of these creatures to be made in honor of and in the likeness of Pharaohs.

the highest of all the mountains thereabout, and the best for pasturage, the herbage being there good; and it had not been before fed upon, because of the opinion men had that God dwelt there. As Moses saw the burning bush fierce and not yet consumed." Josephus records further that, "Moses was frightened at this strange sight but he was still more astonished when the fire uttered a voice, and called to him by name, and spake words to him, by which it signified how bold he had been in venturing to come into a place whither no man had ever come before, because the place was divine."[36] It was the tradition of Orientals to remove their shoes in their home and in all places of worship, in the same way as other cultures remove their hats as a sign of respect. It was a symbol of laying aside of all pollutions from walking in the way of sin, according to Dake.[37] This was a bold move by Moses to go up to a mountain that is divine and that is recognized by others as a place to avoid. Moses experienced the visitation of God Himself, as the Elohim came down and spoke to him out of the burning bush. Moses hid his face and he would not look, for he was afraid to look upon God.

It was an ancient belief that if one saw God, he would die. The Lord heard the cry of the children of Israel and remembered the covenant He had made with them. His covenant was with Abraham, Isaac and Jacob that He would deliver them from the oppression of the Assyrian in Egypt. God had promised that He would bring them to a large land that is filled with milk and honey. This land was presently occupied by the giant tribes: the Canaanites, the Hittites, the Amorites, the Perizzites, the Hivites, and the Jebusities. It was a good land that God was leading them to—a large land, a land of prosperity, and a land of many nations. The Lord wanted these tribes of giants blotted out from the face of the earth. These Canaanites were related to *Acmun* the titan, who named himself *El Eion;* this titan, we discovered, was *Baal* of Phoenicia.

Moses could see from the mention of so many nations the greatness of his mission, for even the armies of Egypt could not conquer these warlike people of Canaan—*the giants.* Moses asks God his *name: "And God said unto Moses, I AM THAT I AM: and he said, Thus shalt thou say unto the children of Israel, I AM hath sent me unto you. And God said moreover unto Moses, Thus shalt thou say unto the children of Israel, the*

LORD God of your fathers, the God of Abraham, the God of Isaac, and the God of Jacob, hath sent me unto you: this is my name for ever, and this is my memorial unto all generations."[38]

This is a very powerful decree by the Almighty God. *"I Am that I Am"* is His name to be revealed. In the Hebrew, *Eheyeh asher Eheyeh,* meaning: "I am that (who or what) I am; or I am the self-existent One, the Eternal, the One who always has been and always will be."[39] This was shortened to *I Am* here, *the Ever-Present* and *Living One.* It is equivalent to *Jehovah the Eternal or the Living God.*

The promise that God made to Abraham, Isaac, and Jacob was a covenant that demonstrates that He is God, the one and the only God, the self-existent God, as proven and demonstrated in the life of Abraham. As church tradition says, it was Nimrod who once put Abraham in the fiery furnace. This happened in his own familiar land among his kindred in Chaldea. The old religion of the titans, tyrants, and giants caused Nimrod to attempt the murder of Abraham. Abraham had deduced through his study of the stars that there must be *one God* above all. The dark prince and his evil religious doctrine could not overcome Abraham. He was preserved supernaturally and came out of the land of the Chaldeans to follow the one and only true God. The covenant that was made with him guaranteed the promise that God would multiply his seed, and from his seed will all the nations of the earth be blessed. This covenant is eternal and continues to bless all of Abraham's seed.

Again the Lord in His empowerment of Moses sent him back to deliver the children of Israel. Moses was eighty years old. God revealed Himself as the Eternal Self-Existent One. As we have ascertained from the old religion of the giants, the six generations of titans are dead and buried. These titans were deified to be gods. They were the offspring of fallen angels and were an abomination to God. The human race has and still deals with these false doctrines that hide behind myth and religion. You will notice a common thread running throughout antiquity which places a superlative efficacy on the power of *names.*

The supernatural power of all kings, monarchs, sovereigns, and Pharaohs was their identification with the gods which empowered them. Moses had to know that His God was above all the gods in Egypt and the known world. His courage came from his total reliance and trust in the God of Abraham, Isaac, and Jacob.

He was well acquainted with the magicians, soothsayers and astrologers of the Egyptian Dynasty. The book of Exodus records the proclamation of Jehovah, *"And I will stretch out my hand, and smite Egypt with all my wonders which I will do in the midst thereof: and after that he will let you go."*[40] Jehovah intended to manifest His mighty power, to prove to Egypt and all other empires and nations that His power and plan for the coming Messiah would be realized. Sin would be put down, man's dominion would be restored, and all false gods that had endeavored to steal the attention, the worship, the resources, the finances, and the dignity of his people, would be crushed and judged for all the empires of the world to see.

Moses tells the Hebrews what to do, *"Every woman shall borrow of her neighbor, and of her that sojourneth in her house, jewels of silver, and jewels of gold, and raiment: and ye shall put them upon your sons, and upon your daughters; and ye shall spoil the Egyptians."*[41]

However this word "borrow" used in the English language and in some of our recorded translations is *inconsistent* with the original thought that God had given. It is very important in retrospect to understand that the Hebrew children had for many years achieved tremendous success. Even in Egypt the covenant was still effective in the lives of the children of Israel. They multiplied and found favor, great wealth, great numbers, and great peace. It was only through the fear of the Assyrian Pharaoh and his son, Merenptah, and their magicians and warlocks, that there had been persecution propagated against the people. They were defrauded from their wealth, from their gold, silver, and all their treasures.

"Lamentations Over the Death of the First-Born in Egypt" Charles Sprague Pearce

God planned that His people would receive just wages for all their hard labor before leaving Egypt.

The Hebrew word *Sha'al* means "to ask, request, to demand or require."[42] Here, it could not possibly mean borrow in the way in which the term is used today. It should be *"ask"* or *"demand."* Josephus, in recording this transference of Egyptian wealth, or the pay back for the wages of the Hebrews, records, "They also honored the Hebrews with gifts; some, in order to get them to depart quickly, and others on account of their neighborhood, and the friendship they had with them."[43] The footnote from Flavius Josephus writings reads, "These large presents made to the Israelites, of vessels of silver and vessels of gold, and raiment,"[44] were as Josephus truly calls them *gifts*—given to them and not lent to them, as our English translation renders. They were spoils *required*. God had ordered the Jews to demand these as their pay and reward during their long and bitter slavery in Egypt. These were as atonements for the lives of the Egyptians. They were the conditions of the Jews' departure, and the Egyptians' deliverance from these terrible judgments which had overtaken them all. These horrific judgements

OPPOSITE

A relief of the bull headed god Khnum, from his temple at Esna. This depiction shows him with four horns and the sun disc.

were finally stopped at the surrender of the Pharaoh. Nor was there any sense in borrowing or lending, when the Israelites were departing out of the Egypt forever.

Exodus makes record of this, *"And the Egyptians were urgent upon the people, that they might send them out of the land in haste; for they said, We be all dead men."*[45] Furthermore, the Scripture states that the Lord's direction regarding the transference of wealth and repayment were wages kept back by fraud from the children of Israel.[46] This implies that the Egyptians had stripped the Israelites of their own jewels, clothing, and other riches which they had when they came into Egypt. Now, they were to get what they needed, and evidently, lack for nothing to travel from Egypt. The spoil here was not to be by raping and violence, but by asking and receiving what was freely given.

The prophet Samuel signifies recovery of that which was taken away by violence.[47] The Egyptians would have refused such request under ordinary circumstances, but God gave Israel favor. Calamities that had befallen the Egyptians in the plagues, and the recent deaths of their first born made the women willing to give what was asked to avoid further loss of family and property. They were glad to give them anything to get rid of them.

It is important to note that this greed, covetousness, persecution, hatred and misuse of the Hebrew people must have been instigated by the dark ruler and his devils. The bull god—the gods that were worshipped locally, regionally, and dynastically—such as *Molech, Apis, Adramelech, Marduke* and *Bel-Merodach,* influenced and mobilized the entire nation of Egypt through the rule of the Assyrian Pharaoh. This Pharaoh and his son, who thought they were gods, were driven by that same dark spirit to stop the seed of the woman prophesied about. They were intent on destroying the entire Hebrew race.

God's plan for people is not only deliverance and freedom from present oppressions but the recovery of everything that was stolen and kept back by fraud. This is a good prelude, relevant to the hour we are occupying now, and displaying the methods of God.

Hebrews says that, *"Through faith he kept the passover, and the sprinkling of blood, lest he that destroyed the firstborn should touch them.*

Apis is one of the most well-known bull gods and was worshiped under that name by both the Egyptians and the Greeks.

By faith they passed through the Red sea as by dry land: which the Egyptians assaying to do were drowned."[48] Jehovah has given clear and specific directions to the Hebrews to follow during their participation of the Passover. They were to partake of it in haste. They were to make sure that one lamb will be completely and totally consumed in one night. A lamb will supply for a whole house. None of it should remain till the morning. The blood should be placed on the door post so that the destroying angel would pass over them. They were to eat it with the staff in their hand, meaning that they were going to be coming out of a land of bondage to a land that God has called them to. Faith mobilized them to pass through the Red Sea as they walked on dry land. As the Egyptians followed to try to recover them, they were buried in the waters.[49]

"The Lord is my strength and song, and He is become my salvation: He is my God, and I will prepare Him an habitation; my father's God, and I will exalt Him. The Lord is a man of war: the Lord is His name,"[50] The children of Israel sang and danced in victory before their God.

Exodus chapter fifteen verse two reads, *"JAH is my strength and my song, and He is become my salvation."* The word in Hebrew for salvation is *Yeshuwah.* It is the same name as *Jesus* or *Joshua*—he has become my deliverance, my victory, my help, my salvation, and my welfare. It is incredible to see that the children of Israel experienced complete and total deliverance from the Egyptians. They were told that the Egyptians you see today, you will see them no more forever. As they were baptized in the Red Sea by passing over on dry land, they came out without a feeble or weak one among them. When they came out with silver and with gold, and with the full experience of the transference of wealth, they immediately acknowledged Jehovah, who is now become *Jesus,* or *Yeshua,* or *Jehoshua.*

He has become their deliverance, their victory, their help, their salvation, and their welfare. Meaning that today, when we come into the saving knowledge of Christ, and experience and accept His full deliverance, we come into an all inclusive experience of provision and preservation that is available to us as decreed in the song in Exodus.

Josephus records very clearly the record of the Egyptian army, in their effort to pursue the Hebrew children and overtake them during

"Delivery of Israel Out of Egypt"
Samuel Colman

OPPOSITE
The weapons of Queen Ahhotep. An accomplished warrior and general, Queen Ahhotep was buried with a large collection of artifacts, including two large battle axes, two long daggers and three medals of military honor.

the crossing of the Red Sea. It reads, "As soon, therefore, as even the whole Egyptian army within it, the sea flowed to its own place, and came down with a torrent raised by storms of wind, and encompassing the Egyptians. Showers of rain also came down from the sky, and dreadful thunders and lightning, with flashes of fire. Thunderbolts also were darted about them. Nor was there any thing which used to be sent by God upon men, as indications of his wrath, which did not happen at this time, for a dark and dismal night oppressed them. And thus did all these men perish, so that there was not one man left to be a messenger of this calamity to the rest of the Egyptians."[51]

Note that some of the very power attributes credited to false gods, such as fighting with thunder bolts, credited to *Zeus,* and other means of control over nature were demonstrated by God magnificently. These were all the things that humanity feared, demonstrated in one moment of judgment by Jehovah Almighty as He literally destroyed the entire army of a super power in one act of divine judgment. Josephus declares, "Of these storms of wind, thunder, and lightning, at this drowning of Pharaoh's army, almost wanting in our copies of Exodus, are but fully extant in that of David's psalms."[52]

The historian further states, "On the next day Moses gathered together the weapons of the Egyptians, which were brought to the camp of the Hebrews by the current of the sea, and the force of the winds resisting it; and he conjectured that this also happened by Divine Providence, so that they might not be destitute of weapons. So when he had ordered the Hebrews to arm themselves with them, he led them to Mount Sinai, to offer sacrifice to God, and to render oblations for the salvation of the multitude, as he was charged to do beforehand."[53]

Whether the weapons of the Egyptians were washed ashore by the mighty current of the sea, aided by the power of God to arm the children of Israel or not, we are not sure. However, it seems very consistent with God's nature to provide all necessary things. Considering the battles that would happen during their sojourning in the wilderness, it makes perfect sense that the Spirit of God could have washed ashore supernaturally the weapons of the Egyptians.

God immediately wanted to converse with Moses. The Scriptures say, *"And the Lord said unto Moses, Come up to me into the mount, and be there: and I will give thee tables of stone, and a law, and commandments which I have written; that thou mayest teach them."*[54] Before this invitation by God for Moses to come up to the mountain with him alone, Moses, Aaron, Nadab Abihu, and seventy of the elders of Israel were invited to dine with God. They saw the God of Israel. They saw, under His feet, paved work of sapphire stone, and as it were, the body of heaven in his clearness.[55]

Seventy-five men were there if Joshua was with Moses as in other places. The witnesses saw God with their eyes wide open and ate and drank with Him, according to Exodus chapter twenty-four. This was a time of corporate communion and fellowship with God. These men were given an eye witness account of His royal majesty. Evidently Moses had gone down from the mountain and the Lord called for Him to come up again so that He would disclose to him the tablets of stone. This was the law and the commandments that Moses was to institute for the children of Israel. Before this history, there was no law for the Hebrews.

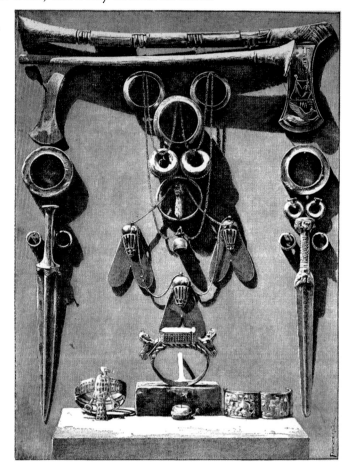

IX

THE ABSENCE OF STRONG LEADERSHIP

Moses went up to the mountain to see God. The sight of the mountain, according to Exodus, was like a devouring fire to all the children of Israel. Moses went into the midst of the cloud and disappeared for forty days. *"And the sight of the glory of the LORD was like devouring fire on the top of the mount in the eyes of the children of Israel. And Moses went into the midst of the cloud, and gat him up into the mount: and Moses was in the mount forty days and forty nights,"* as recorded in the Bible.[1]

The book of Exodus reads, *"And the LORD said unto Moses, Go, get thee down; for thy people, which thou broughtest out of the land of Egypt, have corrupted themselves."*[2]

Moses had spent forty days and forty nights with the Lord, communing with Him and receiving from Him the two tablets of testimony which were written with the finger of God Himself. In addition, he received clear and specific direction on the process of the proper worship of Jehovah Elohim. The *Ten Commandments* were given to Moses to teach the Hebrews the laws of God that would keep them *pure.* Messiah, the Savior of the whole earth, would be born through these chosen people. God wanted to keep them safe from all harm and hurt. Jehovah, knowing the plans of the dark prince and his demons, gave the law of Moses out of the depths of His mercy and compassion.

OPPOSITE
Golden head of the bull god Apis.

In Moses's absence these seditious spirits of devils that had ruled in the ancient empires and greater domains, moved upon the impatient congregation. Using the same gods that the children of Israel were forced to worship in Egypt, the dark ruler tempted them. The same lust and desires that were consistent with that kind of pagan worship came upon their souls. Although they were far removed geographically from Egypt, the dark powers of that land bombarded them with thoughts of fear and confusion. The pressures of these powers must have overtaken the minds of the feeble among them, and stirred them to pressure their leaders. Aaron fell prey to their seditions and determinations.

The children of Israel approached Aaron to demand that he would make *gods* for them to worship. Aaron directed them to break off their earrings of gold from their spouses, sons and daughters; and to bring them to him. All the people broke off their gold and brought a tremendous offering of wealth.[3] Imagine the outlandish amount of gold and silver the Hebrews brought. When they left Egypt, the Scripture says that they spoiled, or *plundered*, the riches of that nation.

This was an idolatrous uprising. The spirit of the prince of darkness will always undertake to actuate among the populace and raise the irresolute to rebellion. The world today seems to be occupied by humanistic persuasions. The population of the world is being dominated by the instigations and control of this dark tyrant that appeal to the obscene nature that rules the unregenerate human. The people came in bitter defiance to have a *god* made for them. In their heart, they returned to Egypt.

Unfortunately, the leadership of Aaron was inept in the absence of Moses. Aaron was constrained by the people to follow their demands. Their actions were in absolute violation of the will of God. They did not refrain from bringing their wealth and treasure—unifying their effort and their desire, to unite in pagan worship and the indulgence of perversion. No doubt the absence of Moses allowed the spirits of devils to instigate the worship of a *god* that they were familiar with. We must understand that many of the children of Israel were being *reacquainted* with *Jehovah Elohim*, the God of their fathers—Abraham, Isaac and Jacob. Some, if not a large percentage, had been involved for many years, in idol worship in the land of their captivity.

The oriental men and women wore earrings, nose rings, finger rings, gold bracelets, chains and other ornaments. They were dripping in gold. They brought their treasures to Aaron who fashioned an idol and sculptured it with a tool. He designed it of gold, in the image of the

chief Egyptian god, a young bull called *Apis*. This deity was worshipped at Memphis near the land of Goshen. The children of Israel worshipped these idols in Egypt. Aaron proclaimed, as recorded in the Bible, *"These be thy gods, O Israel."*[4]

"The Adoration of the Golden Calf" Nicolas Poussin

It is very important to note that Ramesses II and his son, being the Assyrians that conquered Egypt according to our discovery, brought with them the worship of the *bull god Molech* and *Bel-Merodach*— the worship of whom was integrated with that of *Apis*. In *bull worship* men and women yielded themselves to the most vile lecherous acts of deviant perversion. Aaron said these are the *gods* which brought you out of Egypt. He continued to declare that these are the *Elohim*.

Exodus records of the bull god, *"And when Aaron saw it, he built an altar before it; and Aaron made proclamation, and said, To morrow is a feast to the Lord."*[5] He called the golden calf, *Elohim*; and then pronounced a feast unto Jehovah God. Exodus continues, *"And they rose up early on the morrow, and offered burnt offerings, and brought peace offerings; and the people sat down to eat and to drink, and rose up to play."*[6] The religion of the titans, tyrants, and giants continues to undermine all worship intended for Jehovah. The Bible defines *rebellion* as "witchcraft."[7] The religion of Nimrod and his ancestors is embodied in the definition of his name—*"let us rebel."* Aaron misused the true name of God.

Some of the names given to false deities, stolen from God by the dark powers are: *Lord of Heaven* in Babylon, *Baal* in Babylon and Lebanon, *El* of the Phoenicians, *Beluse* of Babylon, *Ninus* of Assyria, *Zeus* of Greece, *Jupiter* of Rome, *Ra* of Egypt, *Vishna* of India, *Pah Ku* of China, *Oden* of Scandinavia, *Gilgamesh* of Mesopotamia, and *Saturn* of Rome.

An Egyptian stele of Apis featuring a winged sun disc.

Different geographical locations worldwide identify this type of dark bullish tyrant by different names and companion images. However, it is the same dark prince who was revealed to me in our prophetic visitation on April 28, 2008—in Tallahassee, Florida. Of course, it is obvious to us that the golden calf was not the *god* that brought the children of Israel out of Egypt. However, in the deficiency of truth and strong leadership, the entire multitude was overtaken by the desires of demonic spirits. They misused the wealth that was brought into their lives to worship the *bull god.* Their memory of Egypt's idolatry caused them to demoralize themselves in eroticism.

This is the first offering ever given after Moses led the Hebrews out of bondage. This misappropriation of wealth was used to fashion the *gods* of Egypt, and led the children of Israel to pay obeisance to them. The fact that Aaron chose to call him in the Hebrew, *Elohim*—a name that was definitive to Jehovah—indicates the backsliding of the entire nation.

"Elohim" is used over two thousand times in the Scripture as the name of Jehovah God.

The children of Israel partook of sensual worship that involved merriment *–to play the whore, to make sport, to laugh, to mock, to corrupt themselves, to commit idolatry, to commit adultery,* and *to commit abomination in the sight of God.* This type of worship is nothing more than the complete and total influence of the religion of the dark prince over the minds and lives of people. It was normal for the pagan nations around this region to practice similar types of worship.

Upon examination of some of the evidence in history and antiquity, we discovered that the *spirit of the bull* and *the image of the bull* is particularized by political authority, governmental rule, illicit sexuality, fertility, economic wealth,

A four horned depiction of Khnum from the Temple of Amun in Kawa, Nubia.

and subterranean powers. Also, these devils and the molten images that the pagans worship present a perplexing evidence of the abominable homosexual rituals associated with the worship cults of this nature.[8]

In the book of Exodus it reads, *"And the Lord said unto Moses, Go, get thee down; for thy people, which thou broughtest out of the land of Egypt, have corrupted themselves."*[9] The Lord knew the overbearing peremptory of the people, and how they had all turned back in their hearts to worship false gods. He aroused to a holy anger and wanted to destroy them; but Moses made intercession for the children of Israel, and reminded God of His covenant with Abraham, Isaac, and Jacob. The meek man, Moses, reminded Almighty God of His promise. Jehovah swore by His Own Self that He would multiply their seed as the stars of heaven.

Moses took the tablets that God had given him and headed down the mountain to his people. Exodus records, *"And when Joshua heard the*

An Egyptian relief showing the Pharaoh Traianus bringing offerings before Horus and Hathor. Horus wears the sun disc and Hathor wears the sun disc and horns.

noise of the people as they shouted, he said unto Moses, There is a noise of war in the camp. And he said, It is not the voice of them that shout for mastery, neither is it the voice of them that cry for being overcome: but the noise of them that sing do I hear. And it came to pass, as soon as he came nigh unto the camp, that he saw the calf, and the dancing: and Moses' anger waxed hot, and he cast the tables out of his hands, and brake them beneath the mount. And he took the calf which they had made, and burnt it in the fire, and ground it to powder, and strewed it upon the water, and made the children of Israel drink of it.[10]

It is a compelling power and responsibility to be an intercessor. Previously, in the mountain, we find Moses pleading the cause of his people. He reminded the Lord of the covenant which was made to Abraham, Isaac, and Jacob. God repented of the evil which He thought to do to the children of Israel. When Joshua heard the noise of the people shout, Joshua thought it was the sound of war in the camp. However, Moses recognized the sound. The Hebrews had backslidden and were celebrating and feasting. He knew the sound of idol worship. He recognized the screams of perversity from his native land. He was accustomed to hearing that revelry when he dwelt in the land of Egypt.

Moses was knowledgeable in all of their magic and occult worship.

When he came to the camp and saw the golden calf and the behavior of all his people, anger rose within him. He threw down the tablets which God had written with His own hand and exercised the authority of His mission. He took the *bull god* which they had made and burnt it in the fire. This image was quite large but he crushed it and ground the gold to fine powder. He poured the gold powder into water and made the children of Israel drink it. The calf was melted, beaten in thin pieces, and ground to powder gold dust, then it was given to them to swallow with water.

Moses saw the nakedness of the people, and how they were exposed. They were uncovered. Aaron fell prey to the demonization of the people and was not able to rule over their selfish desires. Moses immediately called to those who were on the Lord's side and the children of Levi joined him. He sent them out to find the leaders of the rebellion and they killed three thousand men. Moses stopped the insurgence.[11]

The fallen angels that have determined rebellion and war against the God of Heaven are filled with hatred towards His creation. They are covetous of the earth because God has placed us in it. They are jealous of the dominion that we have been given to exercise against them. They want the possessions that God has placed in our hands and within our ability. He gave His people the power to get wealth.[12] These fallen angelic beings are united in one type of purpose, united in one type of determined *"bullheaded"* rebellious act. The dark

A 3,000 year old bull shaped drinking vessel from Mycaenean Crete.

ruler and his forces choose to present themselves among the races of the world from the dawn of time as *"Elohim."* This misrepresents them as part of the family created by God. Their unification of purpose is called by Jesus *the kingdom of darkness.*

According to the book of Mark, *"A kingdom divided against itself cannot stand."*[13] The fallen angelic beings under the rule of satan are captivated by a hatred that is beyond our human comprehension. These beings hate each other, and that hatred is what unifies them. The *bull god* is determined, through the unity of fallen angels, to work together as one force to victimize the human race. Its primary target is destroying covenant by interfering with people's communication with God and with each other. He works through fear and confusion and will stop at nothing to take vengeance upon the Lord—intending on defeating God's creation. These spiritual entities, many times, offer supremacy and prestige to those who seek fame and gain. They back up persons that are in rule and authority, who will cooperate with their agenda. This is why in ancient dynastic times, a man who served as Pharaoh or king was represented in sculpture and in art as a *bull.* The *bull god* endued the monarch with his dark power.

These are the instigators of rebellion. These are the inciters of opposition. These are the propagators of self seeking. These are the gratifiers of the flesh. These are the false gods—fallen angels, unified together under the image of a bull. This dark prince craves the worship that the human race gives so lovingly to Jehovah.

When in the wilderness these false gods were heralded as both "Elohim" and "Jehovah." This fulfilled the very longing of these fallen spirits. It angered the God of Heaven, and moved Moses to deal benevolently with the rebellion in the camp so that the rest of the children of Israel could be spared.

JOSEPHUS CONCERNING ELIJAH "TRIAL OF POWER"

HOW AHAB WHEN HE HAD TAKEN JEZEBEL TO WIFE BECAME MORE WICKED THAN ALL THE KINGS THAT HAD BEEN BEFORE HIM; OF THE ACTIONS OF THE PROPHET ELIJAH, AND WHAT BEFELL NABOTH.

NOW Ahab the king of Israel dwelt in Samaria, and held the government for twenty-two years; and made no alteration in the conduct of the kings that were his predecessors, but only in such things as were of his own invention for the worse, and in his most gross wickedness. He imitated them in their wicked courses, and in their injurious behavior towards God, and more especially he imitated the transgression of Jeroboam; for he worshipped the heifers that he had made; and he contrived other absurd objects of worship besides those heifers; he also took to wife the daughter of Ethbaal, king of the Tyrians and Sidonians, whose name was Jezebel, of whom he learned to worship her own gods. This woman was active and bold, and fell into so great a degree of impurity and madness, that she built a temple to the god of the Tyrians, which they call Belus, and planted a grove of all sorts of trees; she also appointed priests and false prophets to this god. The king also himself had many such about him, and so exceeded in madness and wickedness all [the kings] that went before him.

There was now a prophet of God Almighty, of Thesbon, a country in Gilead, that came to Ahab, and said to him, that God foretold he would not send rain nor dew in those years upon the country but when he should appear. And when he had confirmed this by an oath, he departed into the southern parts, and made his abode by a brook, out of which he had water to drink; for as for his food, ravens brought it to him every day; but when that river was dried up for want of rain, he came to Zarephath, a city not far from Sidon and Tyre, for it lay between them, and this at the command of God, for [God told him] that he should there find a woman who was a widow that should give him sustenance. So when he was not far off the city, he saw a woman that labored with her own hands, gathering of sticks; so God informed him that this was the woman who was to give him sustenance. So he came and saluted her, and desired her to bring him some water to drink; but as she was going so to do, he called to her, and would have her to bring him a loaf of bread also; whereupon she affirmed upon oath that she had at home nothing more than one handful of meal, and a little oil, and that she was going to gather some sticks, that she might knead it, and make bread for herself and her son; after which, she said, they must perish, and be consumed by the famine, for they had nothing for themselves any longer. Hereupon he said, "Go on with good courage, and hope for better things; and first of all make me a little cake, and bring it to me, for I foretell to thee that this vessel of meal and this cruse of oil shall not fail until God send rain." When the prophet had said this, she came to him, and made him the before-named cake; of which she had part for herself, and gave the rest to her son, and to the prophet also; nor did any thing of this fall until the drought ceased. Now Menander mentions this drought in his account of the acts of Ethbaal, king of the Tyrians; where he says thus: "Under him there was a want of rain from the month Hyperberetmus till the month Hyperberetmus of the year following; but when he made supplications, there came great thunders. This Ethbaal built the city Botrys in Phoenicia, and the city Auza in Libya." By these words he designed the want of rain that was in the days of Ahab, for at that time it was that Ethbaal also reigned over the Tyrians, as Menander informs us.

Now this woman, of whom we spake before, that sustained the prophet, when her son was fallen into a distemper till he gave up the ghost, and appeared to be dead, came to the prophet weeping, and beating her breasts with her hands, and sending out such expressions as her passions dictated to her, and complained to him that he had come to her to reproach her for her sins, and that on this account it

"Elijah" by Jose de Ribera

was that her son was dead. But he bid her be of good cheer, and deliver her son to him, for that he would deliver him again to her alive. So when she had delivered her son up to him, he carried him into an upper room, where he himself lodged, and laid him down upon the bed, and cried unto God, and said, that God had not done well, in rewarding the woman who had entertained him and sustained him, by taking away her son; and he prayed that he would send again the soul of the child into him, and bring him to life again. Accordingly God took pity on the mother, and was willing to gratify the prophet, that he might not seem to have come to her to do her a mischief, and the child, beyond all expectation, came to life again. So the mother returned the prophet thanks, and said she was then clearly satisfied that God did converse with him.

After a little while Elijah came to king Ahab, according to God's will, to inform him that rain was coming. Now the famine had seized upon the whole country, and there was a great want of what was necessary for sustenance, insomuch that it was after the recovery of the widow's son of Sarepta, God sent not only men that wanted it, but the earth itself also, which did not produce enough for the horse and the other beasts of what was useful for them to feed on, by reason of the drought. So the king called for Obadiah, who was steward over his cattle, and said to him, that he would have him go to the fountains of water, and to the brooks, that if any herbs could be found for them, they might mow it down, and reserve it for the beasts. And when he had sent persons all over the habitable earth to discover (34) the prophet Elijah, and they could not find him, he bade Obadiah accompany him. So it was resolved they should make a progress, and divide the ways between them; and Obadiah took one road, and the king another. Now it happened that the same time when queen Jezebel slew the prophets, that this Obadiah had hidden a hundred prophets, and had fed them with nothing but bread and water. But when Obadiah was alone, and absent from the king, the prophet Elijah met him; and Obadiah asked him who he was; and when he had learned it from him, he worshipped him. Elijah then bid him go to the king, and tell him that I am here ready to wait on him. But Obadiah replied, "What evil have I done to thee, that thou sendest me to one who seeketh to kill thee, and hath sought over all the earth for thee? Or was he so ignorant as not to know that the king had left no place untouched unto which he had not sent persons to bring him back, in order, if they could take him, to have him put to death?" For he told him he was afraid lest God should appear to him again, and he should go away into another place; and that when the king should send him for Elijah, and he should miss of him, and not be able to find him any where upon earth, he should be put to death. He desired him therefore to take care of his preservation; and told him how diligently he had provided for those of his own profession, and had saved a hundred prophets, when Jezebel slew the rest of them, and had kept them concealed, and that they had been sustained by him. But Elijah bade him fear nothing, but go to the king; and he assured him upon oath that he would certainly show himself to Ahab that very day.

So when Obadiah had informed the king that Elijah was there, Ahab met him, and asked him, in anger, if he were the man that afflicted the people of the Hebrews, and was the occasion of the drought they lay under? But Elijah, without any flattery, said that he was himself the man, he and his house, which brought such sad afflictions upon them, and that by introducing strange gods into their country, and worshipping them, and by leaving their own, who was the only true God, and having no manner of regard to him. However, he bade him go his way, and gather together all the people to him to Mount Carmel, with his own prophets, and those of his wife, telling him how many there were of them, as also the prophets of the groves, about four hundred in number. And as all the men whom Ahab sent for ran away to

the forenamed mountain, the prophet Elijah stood in the midst of them, and said, "How long will you live thus in uncertainty of mind and opinion?" He also exhorted them, that in case they esteemed their own country God to be the true and the only God, they would follow him and his commandments; but in case they esteemed him to be nothing, but had an opinion of the strange gods, and that they ought to worship them, his counsel was, that they should follow them. And when the multitude made no answer to what he said, Elijah desired that, for a trial of the power of the strange gods, and of their own God, he, who was his only prophet, while they had four hundred, might take a heifer and kill it as a sacrifice, and lay it upon pieces of wood, and not kindle any fire, and that they should do the same things, and call upon their own gods to set the wood on fire; for if that were done, they would thence learn the nature of the true God. This proposal pleased the people. So Elijah bade the prophets to choose out a heifer first, and kill it, and to call on their gods. But when there appeared no effect of the prayer or invocation of the prophets upon their sacrifice, Elijah derided them, and bade them call upon their gods with a loud voice, for they might either be on a journey, or asleep; and when these prophets had done so from morning till noon, and cut themselves with swords and lances, according to the customs of their country, and he was about to offer his sacrifice, he bade [the prophets] go away, but bade [the people] come near and observe what he did, lest he should privately hide fire among the pieces of wood. So, upon the approach of the multitude, he took twelve stones, one for each tribe of the people of the Hebrews, and built an altar with them, and dug a very deep trench; and when he had laid the pieces of wood upon the altar, and upon them had laid the pieces of the sacrifices, he ordered them to fill four barrels with the water of the fountain, and to pour it upon the altar, till it ran over it, and till the trench was filled with the water poured into it. When he had done this, he began to pray to God, and to invocate him to make manifest his power to a people that had already been in an error a long time; upon which words a fire came on a sudden from heaven in the sight of the multitude, and fell upon the altar, and consumed the sacrifice, till the very water was set on fire, and the place was become dry.

Now when the Israelites saw this, they fell down upon the ground, and worshipped one God, and called him The great and the only true God; but they called the others mere names, framed by the evil and vile opinions of men. So they caught their prophets, and, at the command of Elijah, slew them. Elijah also said to the king, that he should go to dinner without any further concern, for that in a little time he would see God send them rain.

Accordingly Ahab went his way. But Elijah went up to the highest top of Mount Carmel, and sat down upon the ground, and leaned his head upon his knees, and bade his servant go up to a certain elevated place, and look towards the sea, and when he should see a cloud rising any where, he should give him notice of it, for till that time the air had been clear. When the Servant had gone up, and had said many times that he saw nothing, at the seventh time of his going up, he said that he saw a small black thing in the sky, not larger than a man's foot. When Elijah heard that, he sent to Ahab, and desired him to go away to the city before the rain came down. So he came to the city Jezreel; and in a little time the air was all obscured, and covered with clouds, and a vehement storm of wind came upon the earth, and with it a great deal of rain; and the prophet was under a Divine fury, and ran along with the king's chariot unto Jezreel a city of Issachar (36) [Issaachar].

When Jezebel, the wife of Ahab, understood what signs Elijah had wrought, and how he had slain her prophets, she was angry, and sent messengers to him, and by them threatened to kill him, as he had destroyed her prophets. At this Elijah was affrighted, and fled to the city called Beersheba, which is situate at the utmost limits of the country belonging to the tribe of Judah, towards the land of Edom; and there he left his servant, and went away into the desert. He prayed also that he might die, for that he was not better than his fathers, nor need he be very desirous to live, when they were dead; and he lay and slept under a certain tree; and when somebody awakened him, and he was risen up, he found food set by him and water; so when he had eaten, and recovered his strength by that his food, he came to that mountain which is called Sinai, where it is related that Moses received his laws from God; and finding there a certain hollow cave, he entered into it, and continued to make his abode in it. But when a certain voice came to him, but from whence he knew not, and asked him, why he was come thither, and had left the city? he said, that because he had slain the prophets of the foreign gods, and had persuaded the people that he alone whom they had worshipped from the beginning was God, he was sought for by the king's wife to be punished for so doing. And when he had heard another voice, telling him that he should come out the next day into the open air, and should thereby know what he was to do, he came out of the cave the next day accordingly. When he both heard an earthquake, and saw the bright splendor of a fire; and after a silence made, a Divine

voice exhorted him not to be disturbed with the circumstances he was in, for that none of his enemies should have power over him. The voice also commanded him to return home, and to ordain Jehu, the son of Nimshi, to be king over their own multitude; and Hazael, of Damascus, to be over the Syrians; and Elisha, of the city Abel, to be a prophet in his stead; and that of the impious multitude, some should be slain by Hazael, and others by Jehu. So Elijah, upon hearing this charge,

"Elijah Resuscitating the Son of the Widow of Zarephath" by Louis Hersent

returned into the land of the Hebrews. And when he found Elisha, the son of Shaphat, ploughing, and certain others with him, driving twelve yoke of oxen, he came to him, and cast his own garment upon him; upon which Elisha began to prophesy presently, and leaving his oxen, he followed Elijah. And when he desired leave to salute his parents, Elijah gave him leave so to do; and when he had taken his leave of them, he followed him, and became the disciple and the servant of Elijah all the days of his life. And thus have I despatched the affairs in which this prophet was concerned.

"Slaughter of the Prophets of Baal" by Gustave Dore

Now there was one Naboth, of the city Izar, [Jezreel,] who had a field adjoining to that of the king; the king would have persuaded him to sell him that his field, which lay so near to his own lands, at what price he pleased, that he might join them together, and make them one farm; and if he would not accept of money for it, he gave him leave to choose any of his other fields in its stead. But Naboth said he would not do so, but would keep the possession of that land of his own, which he had by inheritance from his father. Upon this the king was grieved, as if he had received an injury, when he could not get another man's possession, and he would neither wash himself, nor take any food; and when Jezebel asked him what it was that troubled him, and why he would neither wash himself, nor eat either dinner or supper, he related to her the perverseness of Naboth, and how, when he had made use of gentle words to him, and such as were beneath the royal authority, he had been affronted, and had not obtained what he desired. However, she persuaded him not to be cast down at this accident, but to leave off his grief, and return to the usual care of his body, for that she would take care to have Naboth punished; and she immediately sent letters to the rulers of the Israelites [Jezreelites] in Ahab's name, and commanded them to fast and to assemble a congregation, and to set Naboth at the head of them, because he was of an illustrious family, and to have three bold men ready to bear witness that he had blasphemed God and the king, and then to stone him, and slay him in that manner. Accordingly, when Naboth had been thus testified against, as the queen had written to them, that he had blasphemed against God and Ahab the king, she desired him to take possession of Naboth's vineyard on free cost. So Ahab was glad at what had been done, and rose up immediately from the bed whereon he lay to go to see Naboth's vineyard; but

God had great indignation at it, and sent Elijah the prophet to the field of Naboth, to speak to Ahab, and to say to him, that he had slain the true owner of that field unjustly. And as soon as he came to him, and the king had said that he might do with him what he pleased, (for he thought it a reproach to him to be thus caught in his sin,) Elijah said, that in that very place in which the dead body of Naboth was eaten by dogs both his own blood and that of his wife's should be shed, and that all his family should perish, because he had been so insolently wicked, and had slain a citizen unjustly, and contrary to the laws of his country. Hereupon Ahab began to be sorry for the things he had done, and to repent of them; and he put on sackcloth, and went barefoot and would not touch any food; he also confessed his sins, and endeavored thus to appease God. But God said to the prophet, that while Ahab was living he would put off the punishment of his family, because he repented of those insolent crimes he had been guilty of, but that still he would fulfill his threatening under Ahab's son; which message the prophet delivered to the king.

—Flavius Josephus [14]

THE CHILDREN OF ISRAEL IN THE WILDERNESS

Moses led the Hebrews into the desert of Sinai. It is a peninsula that stretches between the horns of the Red Sea; in which lies a wedge of granite and porphyry rocks rising to between eight thousand and nine thousand feet above the sea. Its shape resembles a scalene triangle. These mountains may be divided into two great masses: that of Jebel Serbal, which is six thousand seven hundred and fifty-nine feet high; and the northwest mountains, the central group roughly denoted by the general name Sinai. The Mount of Moses is entitled the pinnacle of *Jebel Musa*. The highest of these mountainous peaks is nine thousand three hundred feet which is the highest point of the whole peninsula.

These mountains are called *Horeb* and *Sinai* synonymously. *Jebel Musa* is regarded in tradition as the place where Moses received the law of God. It is a mountain mass two miles long and one mile wide. It is in full view of the plain of *Rahah*, where the children of Israel were encamped. This is a smooth plain surrounded by mountains. It is approximately two miles long by half a mile wide, embracing four hundred acres of available standing-ground; which makes it into a natural amphitheater by a low semicircular mound about three hundred yards from the foot of the mountain. A great place for Moses to give the Lord's teaching to His people. By actual measurement it contains over two million square yards, and it branches over four million square yards; so that the whole people of Israel, two million in number, would find ample accommodations for seeing and hearing. In addition to this, the air is wonderfully clear, both for seeing and hearing. It was the belief of the Arabs, who conducted Niebuhr that they could make themselves

OPPOSITE
"The Victory of Joshua Over the Amalekites"
Nicolas Poussin

Mount Sinai, where Moses received the law from God.

heard across the Gulf of *Akabah;* a belief fostered by the great distance to which the voice can actually be carried. There is no other place known among all these mountains so well adapted for the purpose of giving and receiving the law, as this rocky pulpit of *Ras Sufsifeh* and the natural amphitheater of the desert plain *Raha.*

It was never *Jehovah Elohim's* intention for the children of Israel to stay in the Sinai Desert for forty-years. We see a coherent definitive sermon delivered by Stephen in the Book of Acts regarding this history. These were the last words he spoke before he was stoned to death by religious zealots, becoming the first martyr of the early church. The Bible reads, *"This is that Moses, which said unto the children of Israel, A prophet shall the Lord your God raise up unto you of your brethren, like unto me; him shall ye hear. This is he, that was in the church in the wilderness with the angel which spake to him in the mount Sina, and with our fathers:*

who received the lively oracles to give unto us: To whom our fathers would not obey, but thrust him from them, and in their hearts turned back again into Egypt, Saying unto Aaron, Make us gods to go before us: for as for this Moses, which brought us out of the land of Egypt, we wot not what is become of him. And they made a calf in those days, and offered sacrifice unto the idol, and rejoiced in the works of their own hands. Then God turned, and gave them up to worship the host of heaven; as it is written in the book of the prophets, O ye house of Israel, have ye offered to me slain beasts and sacrifices by the space of forty years in the wilderness? Yea, ye took up the tabernacle of Moloch, and the star of your god Remphan, figures which ye made to worship them: and I will carry you away beyond Babylon." [1]

The Bible declares that God turned them over to, or gave them up to worship the host of heaven. The Lord clearly states that the children of Israel took up the tabernacle of *Molech* which was the main Ammonite deity that they worshipped in Egypt. They took up also the star of their god *Remphan*. This is the Coptic name for *Saturn; Remphan* is also named *Chiun*. The Lord authenticates that the worship of these images continued to be practiced among the children of Israel all through their journeying in the desert.

The Children of Israel offering sacrifices to Molech.

This Ammonite deity Molech is also recognized as the sun-god, *Ra*. The image itself is hollow: this allows for the *spirit* to enter through an opening in the image's back. *Molech* was a brazen figure, with the body of a man, the head of an ox, and human arms outstretched to receive child sacrifices. He was heated red hot by fire within and the little babies were placed in *Molech's* arms, in the cruelest most murderous methods of worship; while the musicians would beat the loud sounding drums to drown out the cries of dying babies. This *Molech* was also called by his priest, *"lord of heaven."* Again assuming a title that is only authorized to be used regarding our *Lord of Heaven,* Jehovah, and our Lord and Savior, the King—Jesus Christ.

They also carried the figure of *Chiun* or *Remphan* as mentioned in the book of the prophet Amos.[2] These are the Coptic names of *Saturn,* the *"Star god of Babylon."* It was customary for idolaters of all nations to carry small images of their *gods* on their journey and in war. They were enclosed in miniature temples called tabernacles or shrines. The Israelites carried these *gods,* imitating their neighbors, the Moabites and Ammonites. Because they carried these idols, God predicted through Amos that they themselves would go into captivity beyond Damascus into Babylon.[3] The Hebrews were going to be carried away to Babylon because of the *gods* they were worshipping. This prophetic word can be documented in the book of Amos and chapter five; along with the Scripture sited above from the book of Acts.

Jehovah God hates idolatry. They practiced worship of these idols as they carried their little shrines at the same time that they were worshipping Jehovah under the leadership of Moses.

The Saturn hexagon is a persistent hexagonal wave pattern around the North polar vortex. The patterns origin is currently unknown.

According to the writing of Jude the ungodly live a life that resembles the wandering stars. Jude refers to backsliders who are led through life by what they worship and put their trust in.[4] The wandering stars are actual planets. *Saturn* is the sixth planet from the sun and was

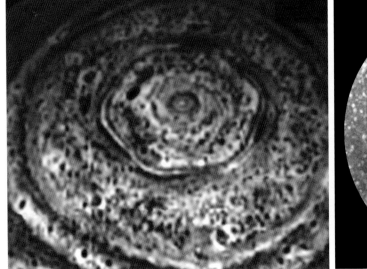
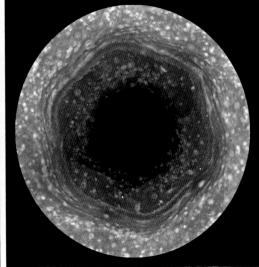

assigned the number "666" according to NASA star maps. *Saturn* is also the origin of the name *Saturday*, which was assigned to a day of the week during the Roman occupation. Concerning the NASA discovery, scientific information states that the pole of the planet Saturn is a six sided hexagon.[5] We have included a photo taken from their satellites.

Moses was a prophet appointed by *Jehovah Elohim;* ministering supernaturally, by the delegated authority given to him as a deliverer of God's chosen people. His ministry is a foreshadowing of the ministry of Christ. Evidently, the enemy's strategy to destroy the *seed* that God had promised, failed. Moses escaped the dark prince, when the command was given by Pharaoh to kill all the newborn sons of the Hebrews.

The leadership of Moses and Joshua brought an emphatic revelation and instruction that would cleanse and purify the Hebrews from the influence of their exposure to pagan gods and heathen nations. Moses said in the book of Deuteronomy that the children of Israel sacrificed to devils[6] and the book of the prophet Ezekiel further declares this same offense.[7]

Subsequently God directly links the carrying away of the children of Israel back to Babylon as judgement for idol worship. We will eventually see that this idol worship was the root cause of them not entering into the Promised Land. Furthermore they were to be carried to Babylon for the worship of the wandering star called *Remphan. Saturn,* the first titan prince to name himself *"king,"* is synonymous with the *"wandering star."* This brings us full circle to the *religion of the titans, tyrants and giants—* still undermining the world today. One more time reminding us of the dark prince and his plan to build another demonic governmental structure—the strategic, *"Invisible Tower of Babel."*

Every time we see these false gods, we see what the book of Galatians calls the works of the flesh. *"Now the works of the flesh are manifest, which are these; Adultery, fornication, uncleanness, lasciviousness, Idolatry, witchcraft, hatred, variance, emulations, wrath, strife, seditions, heresies, Envyings, murders, drunkenness, revellings, and such like: of the which I tell you before, as I have also told you in time past, that they which do such things shall not inherit the kingdom of God."*[8]

It is of consequence to note, that whenever a *god* or *goddess* is revealed in antiquity there is a lunar sign somewhere to be seen. The lunar sign represents the *bull god*. It can be seen as a *crescent moon* worn as a crown, or on their helmets or shields. This image also represents the symbol of the *two-horned bull* of which all false gods are connected. The Egyptian Pharaohs, the Babylonian, and the Assyrian Monarchs can be seen in engravings, images, mosaic portraits, and in golden ornaments wearing this type of headwear. This is their identification with the power of the invisible prince of darkness or the *bull god* as seen from the first century B.C.

Regardless of the many commands of Jehovah Elohim against idolatry, there remains a love of images by many peoples. These images made of earthly materials form a false god that people can see with their eyes and channel their wealth to. Hebrews chapter three and verse nineteen says, *"So we see that they could not enter in because of unbelief."*

The book of Numbers chapter thirteen and verses thirty-two through thirty-three records, *"And they brought up an evil report of the land which they had searched unto the children of Israel, saying, The land, through which we have gone to search it, is a land that eateth up the inhabitants thereof; and all the people that we saw in it are men of a great stature. And there we saw the giants, the sons of Anak, which come of the giants: and we were in our own sight as grasshoppers, and so we were in their sight."*

The armies of the Lord, under the leadership of Moses, were commissioned by the promise of Jehovah God to go and possess the Canaanite land that flows with milk and honey. This was the destination that God promised to them, not the desert of Sinai, but they found *giants* occupying that land. The children of Israel said that the people who dwelt in that land were of great stature; they were giants compared to them. The Lord had shown them earlier that they should not fear the people or their gods.

Jehovah Elohim gave Abraham, Isaac and Jacob this same Canaanite land. The Hebrews made specific reference to giants: they said that the people they had seen in the land were *giants*. Meaning the reputation of *those tribes* and *that race* was well known throughout the world, and far exceeded the boundaries and geographical lines of the land—reaching into the very heart of Egypt itself. So they came back with a slanderous report that described giants in whose presence they seemed to resemble grasshoppers. The people they mentioned were the *Anakims*. All *Anakims* were giants. The historian Josephus speaks of these giants whose bodies were so large and their countenance very different than the sons of men. They were surprising to the sight and the sound; and their voice was terrible to the hearing.[9]

Remember in our study, four hundred years after the flood, that the Lord spoke to Abraham and called him out of Ur to make covenant with him. He led him out of the land of the Chaldeans—the area that would later become the territory of the Assyrians, Babylonians, and the Persians. This exact region of the world today is recognized as *Iraq* and *Iran*—obviously, still ruled and influenced by the same dark powers that hate *Jehovah Elohim* and *Israel*.

When God called Abraham out of his land and established covenant with him, this covenant carried itself through the ministry of Moses; and God delivered the children of Israel from the dominion of the Assyrian Pharaoh. He took them out from under the influence of the worship of the *bull god* that dates back to the tower of Babel. The *bull god* was also the single most recognized *god* among the *Canaanites* of the Promised Land. These giant offspring recognized the *bull god* as their strength and as the procurer of their victory.

Their size and their visage obviously struck terror into the hearts of ten of the twelve spies who recognized them as being *Anakims*. They came back terrified; and reported of the giants who occupied the Promised Land—contesting God's claim and covenant given to the children of Israel. The inhabitants of the Promised Land were all giants. The tribes of the land were *the Kenites, the Kenizzites, the Kadmonites, the Hittites, the Perizzites, the Rephaims, the Amorites, the Canaanites, the Gergashites, the Jebusites, the Hivites, Anakims, Emims, Horims, Avims, Zamzummims, Caphtorims,* and *the Nephilim.* Most of whom were *Gibbor,* meaning *"bullies"* or *"tyrants,"* according to Dake.[10]

The terms *"land of the giants," "valley of the giants,"* and *"remnant of the giants"* are all found in Scripture. Numbers chapter fourteen records, *"And all the children of Israel murmured against Moses and against Aaron: and the whole congregation said unto them, Would God that we had died in the land of Egypt! or would God we had died in this wilderness! And wherefore hath the Lord brought us unto this land, to fall by the sword, that our wives and our children should be a prey? Were it not better for us to return into Egypt?"*[11]

Joshua and Caleb had another report. Joshua and Caleb told the children of Israel that it was an exceedingly good land and if the Lord is with them, the giants are bread for them to eat. All the people wanted to kill Joshua and Caleb; but the Lord appeared in the tabernacle of the congregation and once more Moses interceded to *Jehovah Elohim* for the lives of all Israel. God replied to Moses, *"I have pardoned according to thy word. But as truly as I live, all the earth, shall be filled with the glory of the Lord."*[12] The children of Israel would sojourn in the desert forty years and not go into Canaan, the Promised Land, until another generation

OPPOSITE
A large Hittite cup with the head of a bull. Bulls were one of the most common subjects of Hittite pottery, sculptures and carvings.

REVERSE
The Hittites were skilled at working with both pottery and metals such as bronze.

was raised up. The Lord kept Joshua and Caleb strong. They were to lead the new generation.

History records of Moses that as he was going to embrace Joshua, and was still discoursing with him, all of a sudden a cloud stood over Moses, and he disappeared in a certain valley. Moses wrote in the holy books before then that he died, Josephus concludes, "Lest people should venture to say that, because of his extraordinary virtue, he went to God. Now Moses lived in all one hundred and twenty years; a third part of which time, abating one month, he was the people's ruler; and he died on the last month of the year. He was one that exceeded all men that ever were in understanding, and made the best use of what that understanding suggested to him. He had a very graceful way of speaking and addressing himself to the multitude; and as to his other qualifications, he had such a full command of his passions, as if he had hardly any such in his soul, and only knew them by their names, as rather perceiving them in other men than in himself. He was also such a general of an army as is seldom seen, as well as such a prophet as was never known, and this to such a degree, that whatsoever he pronounced you would think you heard the voice of God himself," according to the histories of Josephus.[13]

An intricate bronze drinking vessel, made in the image of a bull, used in religious rites.

As we know, God made a covenant with Abraham and with His seed that He would bring them out of the land of Egypt and that He would give them an inheritance in the land of Canaan, describing it to be a good land, a large land, land of prosperity, and a land of many nations. This was Jehovah God's definition of the Promised Land. This was the description given by *El Shaddai.* This was where God's people were to inherit as spoken to men of the covenant by the *"True Almighty God."*

Confidence in Him and His ability was present in the lives of Moses, and evident in the life of Joshua and Caleb, whose report of the Promised Land was positive. They said that they were well able to take it. Their desire to dispossess the giants from their land was immediate. God recognized that they had another spirit, implying that the ten spies full of fear were under the influence of the wrong spirit. Remember who the children of Israel were worshipping along with Jehovah

in the desert: *Molech* and the *'wandering star'*, *Remphan.* These were the *gods* of their enemies. The influence of these gods, which empowered the giants, struck fear into their hearts, causing them to be afraid of the giants and their gods, rather than believe the promise giver—*Jehovah Elohim.* Fearing the *giants* would mean fearing their *god.*

Goliath slain by David was about thirteen feet tall. The revelation we have of giants in Scripture gives us a clear Biblical picture of the origin of all false gods. These giant nations, made up of beings of great stature, struck fear in the heart of the spies who brought back slanderous reports based on the power, the size, the reputation, and the *god* of these giant peoples. To fear them meant to fear their gods. Acknowledging their power meant falling prey to worshipping their *gods. So we see that they could not enter in because of unbelief.*[14]

The children of Israel carried the tabernacle of *Molech,* as we recognize. They were mindful of the "star god," *Remphan.* They were still under the influence of the false religious worship of *Apis* in Egypt. They were still cognizant of of the fact that Pharaoh, the Assyrian king *Ramesses,* and his son were also synonymous with the "god" they serve. They feared the giants in the land by associating them with the "gods" the giants served. That is the conclusion of why they would be carried away into captivity according to Amos chapter five and verse twenty-seven.

As a result of their disobedience to invade the Promised Land, they were judged to wander in the wilderness. Not possessing the land of the giants, for fear of their fortified cities and the giant tribes within Canaan, they continued the secret observance of the "chief wandering star" *Saturn*—carrying about the images of *Molech* of Ammon and *Moab.*

After forty years in the wilderness of Sinai, Joshua, and Caleb conquered Canaan. Joshua ruled for thirty years and died at one hundred and ten years old.

JOSEPHUS CONCERNING DAVID'S MIGHTY MEN

HOW THE HEBREWS WERE DELIVERED FROM A FAMINE WHEN THE GIBEONITES HAD CAUSED PUNISHMENT TO BE INFLICTED FOR THOSE OF THEM THAT HAD BEEN SLAIN; AS ALSO, WHAT GREAT ACTIONS WERE PERFORMED AGAINST THE PHILISTINES BY DAVID, AND THE MEN OF VALOR ABOUT HIM.

AFTER this, when the country was greatly afflicted with a famine, David besought God to have mercy on the people, and to discover to him what was the cause of it, and how a remedy might be found for that distemper. And when the prophets answered, that God would have the Gibeonites avenged whom Saul the king was so wicked as to betray to slaughter, and had not observed the oath which Joshua the general and the senate had sworn to them: If, therefore, said God, the king would permit such vengeance to be taken for those that were slain as the Gibeonites should desire, he promised that he would be reconciled to them, and free the multitude from their miseries. As soon therefore as the king understood that this it was which God sought, he sent for the Gibeonites, and asked them what it was they should have; and when they desired to have seven sons of Saul delivered to them to be punished, he delivered them up, but spared Mephibosheth the son of Jonathan. So when the Gibeonites had received the men, they punished them as

they pleased; upon which God began to send rain, and to recover the earth to bring forth its fruits as usual, and to free it from the foregoing drought, so that the country of the Hebrews flourished again. A little afterward the king made war against the Philistines; and when he had joined battle with them, and put them to flight, he was left alone, as he was in pursuit of them; and when he was quite tired down, he was seen by one of the enemy, his name was Achmon, the son of Araph, he was one of the sons of the giants. He had a spear, the handle of which weighed three hundred shekels, and a breastplate of chain-work, and a sword. He turned back, and ran violently to slay [David] their enemy's king, for he was quite tired out with labor; but Abishai, Joab's brother, appeared on the sudden, and protected the king with his shield, as he lay down, and slew the enemy. Now the multitude were very uneasy at these dangers of the king, and that he was very near to be slain; and the rulers made him swear that he would no more go out with them to battle, lest he should come to some great misfortune by his courage and boldness, and thereby deprive the people of the benefits they now enjoyed by his means, and of those that they might hereafter enjoy by his living a long time among them.

Bronze breast plate and shield, typical of the kind used during the time of David.

When the king heard that the Philistines were gathered together at the city Gazara, he sent an army against them, when Sibbechai the Hittite, one of David's most courageous men, behaved himself so as to deserve great commendation, for he slew many of those that bragged they were the posterity of the giants, and vaunted themselves highly on that account, and thereby was the occasion of victory to the Hebrews. After which defeat, the Philistines made war again; and when David had sent an army against them, Nephan his kinsman fought in a single combat with the stoutest of all the Philistines, and slew him, and put the rest to flight. Many of them also were slain in the fight. Now a little while after this, the Philistines pitched their camp at a city which lay not far off the bounds of the country of the Hebrews. They had a man who was six cubits tall, and had on each of his feet and hands one more toe and finger than men naturally have. Now the person who was sent against them by David out of his army was Jonathan, the son of Shimea, who fought this man in a single combat, and slew him; and as he was the person who gave the turn to the battle, he gained the greatest reputation for courage therein. This man also vaunted himself to be of the sons of the giants. But after this fight the Philistines made war no more against the Israelites.

And now David being freed from wars and dangers, and enjoying for the future a profound peace, composed songs and hymns to God of several sorts of metre; some of those which he made were trimeters, and some were pentameters. He also made instruments of music, and taught the Levites to sing hymns to God, both on that called the sabbath day, and on other festivals. Now the construction of the instruments was thus: The viol was an instrument of ten strings, it was played upon with a bow; the psaltery had twelve musical notes, and was played upon by the fingers; the cymbals were broad and large instruments, and were made of brass. And so much shall suffice to be spoken by us about these instruments, that the readers may not be wholly unacquainted with their nature.

Now all the men that were about David were men of courage. Those that were most illustrious and famous of them for their actions were thirty-eight; of five of whom I will only relate the performances, for these will suffice to make manifest the virtues of the others also; for these were powerful enough to subdue countries, and conquer great nations. First, therefore, was Jessai, the son of Achimaas, who frequently leaped upon the troops of the enemy, and did not leave off fighting till he overthrew nine hundred of them. After him was Eleazar, the son of Dodo, who was with the king at Arasam. This man, when once the Israelites were under a consternation at the multitude of the Philistines, and were running away, stood alone, and fell upon the enemy, and slew many of them, till his sword clung to his band by the blood he had shed, and till the Israelites, seeing the Philistines retire by his means, came

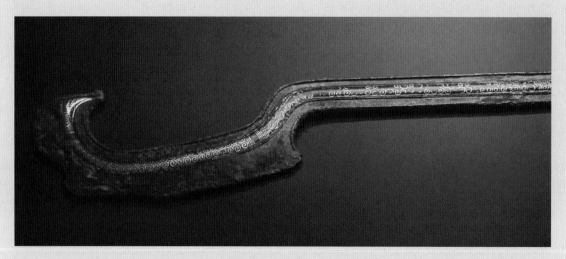

Shown above, a Khopesh is a hybrid sword/battle axe used mainly the Egyptians and the Canaanites prior to 1300 B.C.

down from the mountains and pursued them, and at that time won a surprising and a famous victory, while Eleazar slew the men, and the multitude followed and spoiled their dead bodies. The third was Sheba, the son of Ilus. Now this man, when, in the wars against the Philistines, they pitched their camp at a place called Lehi, and when the Hebrews were again afraid of their army, and did not stay, he stood still alone, as an army and a body of men; and some of them he overthrew, and some who were not able to abide his strength and force he pursued. These are the works of the hands, and of fighting, which these three performed. Now at the time when the king was once at Jerusalem, and the army of the Philistines came upon him to fight him, David went up to the top of the citadel, as we have already said, to inquire of God concerning the battle, while the enemy's camp lay in the valley that extends to the city Bethlehem, which is twenty furlongs distant from Jerusalem. Now David said to his companions, "We have excellent water in my own city, especially that which is in the pit near the gate," wondering if any one would bring him some of it to drink; but he said that he would rather have it than a great deal of money. When these three men heard what he said, they ran away immediately, and burst through the midst of their enemy's camp, and came to Bethlehem; and when they had drawn the water, they returned again through the enemy's camp to the king, insomuch that the Philistines were so surprised at their boldness and alacrity, that they were quiet, and did nothing against them, as if they despised their small number. But when the water was brought to the king, he would not drink it, saying, that it was brought by the danger and the blood of men, and that it was not proper on that account to drink it. But he poured it out to God, and gave him thanks for the salvation of the men. Next to these was Abishai, Joab's brother; for he in one day slew six hundred. The fifth of these was Benaiah, by lineage a priest; for being challenged by [two] eminent men in the country of Moab, he overcame them by his valor, Moreover, there was a man, by nation an Egyptian, who was of a vast bulk, and challenged him, yet did he, when he was unarmed, kill him with his own spear, which he threw at him; for he caught him by force, and took away his weapons while he was alive and fighting, and slew him with his own weapons. One may also add this to the forementioned actions of the same man, either as the principal of them in alacrity, or as resembling the rest. When God sent a snow, there was a lion who slipped and fell into a certain pit, and because the pit's mouth was narrow it was evident he would perish, being enclosed with the snow; so when he saw no way to get out and save himself, he roared. When Benaiah heard the wild beast, he went towards him, and coming at the noise he made, he went down into the mouth of the pit and smote him, as he struggled, with a stake that lay there, and immediately slew him. The other thirty-three were like these in valor also.

—Flavius Josephus[15]

BABYLON

King Nebuchadnezzar destroyed Solomon's temple in Jerusalem approximately five hundred and eight-five years before Christ. This was around eight hundred years after Joshua conquered the Promised Land. Hundreds of years of history pass—from the rule of the judges of Israel; to her first kings, Saul then David; Assyria becomes a world empire, and Babylon takes the world from Assyria—yet subsequently the covenant between the Lord and his people is undisturbed.

After the siege of Jerusalem, Nebuchadnezzar returned quickly to Babylon, taking precious vessels from the house of *Jehovah Elohim*. He brought them to the treasure stores of the great temple of his god *Bel*. This chief god of Babylon, *Bel,* was synonymous with the *"Star god Saturn," Bel Merodach, Marduke, Molech* and others, as we have shown through our study. All were the same *god* with slight differences in image and worship. The great temple of *Bel* was where the Babylonian army would bring the spoil and the treasures that they had acquired from the nations that they conquered.

His generals brought all the Hebrews that they had captured to Babylon, bringing Daniel and his companions along. According to Daniel chapter one, Nebuchadnezzar's generals brought the children of Israel and chose from them those who were princes, without blemish, handsome in appearance, well educated, skillful in knowledge, and proficient in sciences. They were defined and polished so that they may be able to stand before the sovereign. They were the best of the captured Hebrews. They were people of understanding who were cunning, and had the ability of learning.

OPPOSITE
"Babylon" Frantisek Kupka

"And the king appointed them a daily provision of the king's meat, and of the wine which he drank: so nourishing them three years, that at the end thereof they might stand before the king."[1] The book of Daniel continues, *"Now among these were of the children of Judah, Daniel, Hananiah, Mishael, and Azariah: Unto whom the prince of the eunuchs gave names: for he gave unto Daniel the name of Belteshazzar; and to Hananiah, of Shadrach; and to Mishael, of Meshach; and to Azariah, of Abednego."[2]* We will see that these Hebrews, who were chosen because of their potential to be trained and fashioned in the knowledge of Babylon, never ceased to worship *Jehovah*. They complying to *Jehovah's* law, by even refusing to partake of the food of the king's table.

Babylon supplied training in mathematics, anatomy and astronomy. Daniel was no doubt trained in all these sciences. The ancient inscriptions show that there was a special palace school with elaborate arrangements for education. The word learning is *sepher*, meaning *"book, literature, history, and records."* Babylon had huge libraries with books classified on all subjects which could be secured. There was a special department in the palace to train these promising aristocrats.

Babylon had access to all the knowledge of Egypt. Many theologians call this period of history, *Neo-Babylon:* meaning *"New Babylon."* We have studied the wealth of knowledge that dates back to

Abraham and Chaldea after the flood. We have also seen the dark knowledge of certain arts given from fallen angels to their offspring. These titan princes were knowledgeable in all things necessary to build advanced edifices and ziggurats. We have traced the origins of advanced knowledge to the land of Shinar, east of the Euphrates.[3] Nebuchadnezzar conquered Egypt and inherited the knowledge of both empires.

Daniel's name means *"God is Judge"* in Hebrew.[4] The Babylonians renamed him *Belteshazzar,* meaning *"preserve thou O Bel his life"* or *'prince of Bel.'* Daniel did not like the name the Babylonians gave, and chose to continue to be called Daniel. For this name *Belteshazzar* related to the chief deity of Babylon, *Bel Merodach* or *Bel.*

Hananiah meaning *"gift of the Lord"* was renamed *Shadrach,* meaning *"command of Aku,"* the *moon god.* Again we see the *lunar god* which is directly linked to the *"bull god"* and related by the *crescent moon*—resembling the two horns. This is the personification of the devil, and the the instigator of the works of the flesh.

It was obvious that the great empire of Babylon was assimilating the cream of the crop from among the Hebrew princes. They were renaming them in hope of recruiting them for the benefit and the progress of their kingdom and their culture.

Mishael, whose name means *"who is what God is,"* was renamed *Meshach*—*"who is as Aku."* Again we see the *moon god* referenced here in correlation with the *bull god. Azariah,* meaning *"whom Jehovah helps"* was renamed *Abed-nego, "servant of Nego,"* or *Nebo*: the *god* of science and literature. This is again related to the Babylonian deity. Giving different names to captives or foreign slaves was a sign of putting them under subjection, preparing them for a special and lengthy training course by the ruler of that kingdom.

Daniel received favor from the Babylonians because he could interpret dreams, and the gifting of God was upon him. Daniel was exalted and promoted by the rulers. His righteous life contributed to the witness of Jehovah. Nebuchadnezzar dreamed a dream and his spirit was troubled. He could not go back to sleep that night. Nebuchadnezzar was

An engraving on an onyx stone eye from a Marduk that depicts Nebuchadnezzar and reads, "In honor of Merdoch, his lord, Nebuchadnezzar, King of Babylon in his lifetime had this made."

OPPOSITE
A Sumerian-Akkadian Lexicon, Volume 16 of a 24 volume encyclopedia from Uruk. It was compiled in the old Babylonian period from pre-existing texts, dating back to 3000 B.C.

One of approximately 120 glazed brick lions lining the walls of the processional way leading to the temple of Ishtar.

a warrior, a soldier; he did acts that resembled the accomplishments of heroes. He was *"god king"* whose dominion extended all the way beyond the region of present day Iran, Iraq, Syria, Judea, Libya, and reached into Mauritania in Africa. This king built one of the most amazing empires on the planet. Yet, he could still not sleep because of a dream. He could not sleep because the dream was from *Jehovah Elohim.*

Nebuchadnezzar commanded all of his magicians, astrologers, sorcerers, and the Chaldeans to come and stand before him. Some of these men could speak in different dialects and were trained in all foretelling arts. The Chaldean spoke to the king in Syriac, an Aramaic type of dialect. He told the king to tell them the dream and that they would show him the interpretation.

The king told the Chaldean that he wanted them to not only interpret the dream but he wanted them to tell him exactly *what* he dreamt. The magicians, astrologers, sorcerers, and the Chaldean told Nebuchadnezzar that this has never happened before. They shared with the king that he was supposed to tell them the dream first and then they would interpret its meaning. The king was so angry that he shouted, "Cut them into pieces and make their houses as dung hills." Daniel spoke boldly and asked the king for some time. He immediately went to his house and told Hananiah, Mishael, and Asariah, his companions, the king's demands. All the wise men in Babylon were going to perish if Daniel did not hear from the Lord.[5]

Jehovah Elohim reveals the deep and secret things, He knows what is in the darkness and all light dwells in Him. Daniel gives thanks to God for wisdom and might because the Lord showed him the king's dream. Daniel quickly returns to Nebuchadnezzar and he says, *"Thou, O king, sawest, and behold a great image. This great image, whose brightness was excellent, stood before thee; and the form thereof was terrible. This image's head was of fine gold, his breast and his arms of silver, his belly and his thighs of brass, His legs of iron, his feet part of iron and part of clay. Thou sawest till that a stone was cut out without hands, which smote the image upon his feet that were of iron and clay, and brake them to pieces. Then was the iron, the clay, the brass, the silver, and the gold, broken to pieces together, and became like the chaff of the summer threshingfloors; and the wind carried them away, that no place was found for them: and the stone that smote the image became a great mountain, and filled the whole earth."*[6]

Daniel interpreted the dream and first tells Nebuchadnezzar, *"Thou, O king, art a king of kings: for the God of heaven hath given thee a kingdom, power, and strength, and glory."*[7] He said, You are the head of gold. You

One of the glazed brick bulls on the Ishtar gate itself, an enormous blue arching doorway covered in brick inlays of dragons and bulls.

are the pure Babylonian government. You are allowed by God to rule *"wheresoever the children of men dwell, the beasts of the field and the fowls of the heaven hath he given into thine hand, and hath made thee ruler over them all. Thou art this head of gold."*[8]

Daniel explained that after you there is going to come the shoulders, and they are going to be made out of silver. The next government will be inferior to yours. The one after that will be made out of brass and shall rule over all the earth. And the fourth kingdom will be as strong iron. The iron will break in pieces and subdue all things. And where you saw the feet and toes were part iron and part clay, so will the kingdom be partly strong and partly broken. When you saw the iron mix with the miry clay, they will mingle themselves with the seed of men; but they will not cleave one to another, even as iron is not mixed with clay.[9]

"And in the days of these kings shall the God of heaven set up a kingdom, which shall never be destroyed: and the kingdom shall not be left to other people, but it shall break in pieces and consume all these kingdoms, and it shall stand for ever," as recorded in the book of Daniel.[10]

The partially reconstructed ruins of Babylon.

Then the king Nebuchadnezzar fell on the ground and worshipped Daniel, and said, *"Of a truth it is, that your God is a God of gods, and a Lord of kings, and a revealer of secrets, seeing thou couldest reveal this secret. Then the king made Daniel a great man, and gave him many great gifts, and made him ruler over the whole province of Babylon, and chief of the governors over all the wise men of Babylon"*[11] Daniel requested the help of Shadrach, Meshach, and Abednego, and they were appointed over the affairs of the province of Babylon. The lives of all the wise men were spared.

Josephus records, "Nebuchadnezzar erected elevated places for walking, of stone, and made it resemble mountains, and built it so that it might be planted with all sorts of trees. He also erected what was called a pensile paradise, because his wife was desirous to have things like her own country, she having been bred up in the palaces of Media."

Megasthenes, also, in his fourth book of his *Accounts of India*, mentions of these things, and thereby endeavors to show that this, King Nebuchadnezzar, exceeded *Hercules* in fortitude, and in the greatness of his actions; for he saith that he conquered a great part of Libya and Iberia.[12]

Also Diocles, in the second book of his *Accounts of Persia*, mentions this ruler; as does Philostrates, in his *Accounts both of India and of Phoenicia,* saying that this monarch besieged Tyre thirteen years, while at the same time Ethbaal reigned at Tyre.[13] Josephus also mentioned that King Nebuchadnezzar's son who succeeded him was called *Evil-Merodach.*[14] From this record in Josephus, it seems factual that King Nebuchadnezzar was a man of extraordinary or supernatural achievements. He must have been an avid follower and worshipper of *Bel-Merodach,* the Babylonian *god.* His son's name was *Evil-Merodach.* It is very possible that he had procured the supernatural aid of the dark prince to empower the kingdom of Babylon. It is also probable that this king was supernaturally driven to accomplish such feats—feats that would gain him mention in antiquities, as exceeding *Hercules* in accomplishments.

We must remember that it was not abnormal for kings and monarchs to be named interchangeably with the *god* that they served. This would unite them with that *god* so that they could be considered to be *"god himself."*

This Nebuchadnezzar built an image of gold. The image was made out of pure gold and seemed to be at least one hundred and twenty-feet high and twelve and one half foot wide. It is impossible to know the certainty of the nature of this image. His shape and form is unknown, but it was common practice in Assyria, Babylon, and Egypt for the Pharaoh, the King, and the Monarch to be regarded as a *god.*

It is possible, considering Nebuchadnezzar's worldwide reputation and the accomplishments and the achievements that we see attributed to him through historians in antiquity, that this image may have been either a golden image of the king himself, or a form that conjoined or mingled the king and *Nebu,* the *god* of Babylon.

OPPOSITE

"A Naval Action During the Siege of Tyre" Andre Castaigne

It is also important to recognize that treasures and wealth are intricately involved in any form of worship. Imagine a statue and image—molten and graven; made of pure gold; one hundred twenty-five foot high, and twelve and one half foot wide; erected specifically for the purpose of inciting an entire population to exercise worship. This statue represented the wealth of an empire, the status of a king, the power of a god, and the *attention of the people.*

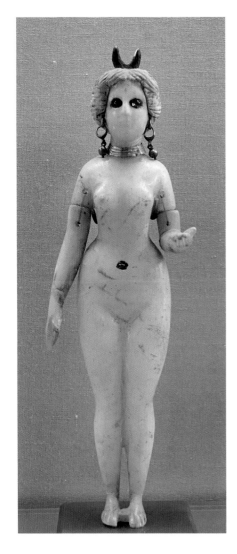

A horned Babylonian statue of Ishtar, also known as Astarte and Ashtoreth (the two horned)

Worship and *"things of worth"* always go together. *Jehovah Elohim* is the Provider the Supplier. He is the Multiplier, and the Nourisher of His people. When we worship Him with our talent, our treasures, our abilities and strength that He gives to us; He in turn, releases His help and His power, to promote, help, and bless us. It is His will that we occupy the land that He has promised us and that we keep the victory that is given to us. *Jehovah Elohim* wants us to always be willing and obedient so that we can eat of the good of the land.

This image that King Nebuchadnezzar made was put in a certain plain called Dura in the province of Babylon. He also informed princes, governors, captains, judges, treasures, counselors, sheriffs and rulers of the provinces to come and be part of the initiation. King Nebuchadnezzar wanted the acknowledgement of this imposing image to cause all people to worship together in the obedience that he felt belonged to this golden *god.*

King Nebuchadnezzar informed those in charge of the treasure houses! Notice again the involvement of the wealth of the empire in the acknowledgement of a particular religious system. I believe that as we study and meditate on the revelations revealed in this book, we will see the prince of darkness and his strategies exposed; his covetous, tyrannical methods always crave the wealth and the worship of people. As we see this truth brought to light, our worship to the Lord will be free to include our finances. We will be able to participate in the greatest transference of wealth the world has ever known—even at a time when nations, kingdoms and global economies are in the midst of turbulent crisis.

This is a super power. Babylon at this time represented a one world government, the single foremost world power, uniting the religion, the ruler, and the wealth, in one solid union. This brawn is backed up by the power of military forces that will stop at nothing to prove the supremacy and potency of their form of government.

King Nebuchadnezzar also invited the rulers of counselors who were law givers and judges and supreme masters and magistrates, called sheriffs; state and civil officers; and various wise men. It is important to know that they were heralded and introduced to represent every branch and every aspect of Nebuchadnezzar's kingdom and society. They were to participate in this great and historic time of worship as they acknowledge this golden image.

Music was to be played: a deep horn with a hollow sound was to be implemented, a wind instrument with a strong sound, and other various musical pieces. Drums were also to be used. As they released the music, everyone who heard it was commanded to bow and to pay homage to this golden image.

Behind the scenes, those of us who understand spiritual matters know that Bel, the god of Babylon, is a dark spiritual force, not a golden statue or an image. He is a spiritual force, a principality; as proven to us in the recorded conversations between Daniel and the angel of the Lord. The battle that was waged over Daniel's prayer was fought between the *Prince of Persia, Gabriel* and *Michael.* These are angels waging war with principalities and powers.[15]

According to the book of Ephesians, *"For we wrestle not against flesh and blood, but against principalities, against powers, against the rulers of the darkness of this world, against spiritual wickedness in high places."*[16] When we acknowledge the empowerment of Nebuchadnezzar's golden statue, we must recognize that as the music was released, a tremendous

Selene, the Greek goddess of the moon, depicted here with the moon on her head as horns.

demonic spiritual force was pressed upon the mind, the will, and the emotions of the people, virtually compelling them to bow. These people represented the conquered nations that *Nebuchadnezzar's* Babylon had overthrown and subjugated. There must have been a spiritual force that drove and compelled them to sense that this statue indeed represented a superhuman power. There was a dark spiritual force that drove them to obey the commands of the king.

Nebuchadnezzar believed he was the incarnation of *Nimrod*. By this time Nimrod had been deified as a hero hunter. His symbol was a man lion or a human-headed lion with eagle's wings, named *Nergal*. He was an Assyrian deity entitled *"God of the Battles,"* or *"God of chase."* In dynastic times, as we know, Pharaoh could be represented as a lion or a bull with the face of a man. Nebuchadnezzar was enchanted by images of both. *Adremelech* of Assyria was identical with *Molech* with the body of a man and a head of a calf. Bulls with the face of this obsessed monarch covered the gates of Babylon, appearing as human headed winged bulls carved in stone.

Human sacrifice was conducted to this *god* as we discovered earlier. Also, the *Sphinx* of Egypt had the face of the Pharaoh, and the body of a lion. Nebuchadnezzar had conquered Egypt. These images represent both the power of *Bel,* the *god* of Babylon, as well as maintain the deity of the king himself. These human headed winged bulls were stationed on the gates, on the walls of temples all over Babylon to guard the empire and to represent the power of their *god* and the unquestionable rule of their Nebuchadnezzar.

The command to bow down to the golden image was proclaimed to all. Princes, governors, captains, judges, treasurers, counselors, sheriffs, and rulers of provinces all came to the dedication and bowed at the sound of the musical blast.

However, the three Hebrew children would not bow, nor would they worship the *gods of the king*. They were immediately accused that they gave no regard to the king, and that they did not serve his *gods* and did not worship the golden image.

"There are certain Jews whom thou hast set over the affairs of the province of Babylon, Shadrach, Meshach, and Abednego; these men,

O king, have not regarded thee: they serve not thy gods, nor worship the golden image which thou hast set up," as recorded in the book of Daniel.[17] Because of their defiance to the king and their allegiance to Jehovah, they would have to be punished. However, the Bible says, *"I am the LORD thy God, which have brought thee out of the land of Egypt, out of the house of bondage. Thou shalt have no other gods before me. Thou shalt not make unto thee any graven image, or any likeness of any thing that is in heaven above, or that is in the earth beneath, or that is in the water under the earth. Thou shalt not bow down thyself to*

One of the two statues flanking the entrance to the throne room of King Sargon II, it depicts a creature with the winged body of a bull and the head of a man.

A painting depicting the three Hebrew children unharmed within the fiery furnace, by Franz Joseph Hermann.

them, nor serve them: for I the LORD thy God am a jealous God, visiting the iniquity of the fathers upon the children unto the third and fourth generation of them that hate me."[18]

The children of Israel, Shadrach, Meschach, and Abednego, were in direct obedience to the word of God recorded in the law of Moses. God acknowledges or identifies Himself as the Lord our God, and He declares that we should not have any other gods before Him. This is referred to in the Pentateuch many times because of the consequence of this particular sin.

Jehovah Elohim gave the law to Moses to protect the children of Israel and all who believe from falling prey to deception from pretentious devils. The Lord further said that the human race should never make any graven image to worship. The word is *pesel*, meaning to *"hew, engrave, or sculpture."*[19] This command forbids making any kind of idol, and prohibits every kind of idolatry.

Of course God is not against creativity; He is the Creator of all. Look at the sky or a beautiful flower, and you will see God's love. *Worship* is another matter. The fallen angel—the dark prince—covets the worship of people. So He commanded that there shall be no graven image made in any likeness of the things in heaven above, the earth beneath, or under the earth.

So the Hebrew children, Shadrach, Meschach, and Abednego would not defy the Lord and were sentenced to death in the fiery furnace. Because of the fury of the king, the furnace was heated seven times hotter than before. Tradition says that the flames reached over one hundred feet high. These three Hebrews were not merely thrown into the furnace; they were dressed in flammable clothing which would make them burn faster and longer. They were to be made an example of the kind of judgment that would befall anyone who would dare to disregard the king. The Babylonians wore a tunic of linen reaching down to their feet, with a woolen tunic over that, and a white short cloak. They also wore turbans on their heads and all of these clothes were extremely flammable.

The violence of the flame should have slain them; however, it slew the men that threw them in. The Hebrews fell down as they were bound in the midst of the fiery furnace. In the *Song of the Three Holy Children* in the Apocrypha, it is stated that the servants of Nebuchadnezzar kept throwing rosin, pitch, tow, and small kindling wood to feed the furnace to strengthen the flames. However, there was an intervention by a superhuman being. According to the book of Daniel, *"Then Nebuchadnezzar the king was astonished, and rose up in haste, and spake, and said unto his counsellors, Did not we cast three men bound into the midst of the fire? They answered and said unto the king, True, O king. He answered and said, Lo, I see four men loose, walking in the midst of the fire, and they have no hurt; and the form of the fourth is like the Son of God."*[20]

This was an astonishing sight that took place in the presence of a mighty monarch, whose deeds and acts of supreme rule were thought to have exceeded those of *Hercules.* He was certain that such a hot flame would instantly slay these three bound, powerless Hebrew children. He was certain that his *gods,* that had empowered the Babylonian Empire, would become the superpower of a one world government. Nebuchadnezzar had no doubt that these flames would be more than enough to overcome the Hebrews who were in allegiance and chose to worship *Jehovah God.*

The three Hebrews had claimed to serve the *"True and Living God."* Their bodies were immune to the fire and not even a hair on their head was burnt. Their garments were not burnt and they did not smell like smoke. Nebuchadnezzar knew that he had seen *"the Son of God."* He had never seen such preserving power. He was not ignorant of supernatural works or supernatural apparitions. His entire Kingdom depended on his *gods,* and now he saw *"One"* more powerful than any other. The Hebrew children confessed that God had sent His angel. God delivers those who trust Him.

A relief from the North wall of the palace of King Sargon II depicting a winged deity.

The angels of God were known to appear to kings, pharaohs, and monarchs during their history. These fables and legions were passed down generation to generation by word of mouth and later by written words. Nebuchadnezzar believed *Nergal* was a *god.* He believed *Bel Merodach* was a *god.* He believed himself to be a *god.*

"Therefore I make a decree, That every people, nation, and language, which speak any thing amiss against the God of Shadrach, Meshach, and Abednego, shall be cut in pieces, and their houses shall be made a dunghill: because there is no other God that can deliver after this sort. Then the king promoted Shadrach,

Meshach, and Abednego, in the province of Babylon," as recorded in the book of Daniel.[21]

Had King Nebuchadnezzar not been recognized as a *god* himself—by virtue of his allegiance and identification with *Bel,* the *god* of Babylon—he could not have made such a decree that exalted *Jehovah* of Israel above the *god* of Babylon. But by speaking

A pair of winged deity from the palace of Ashurnasirpal II.

that, he made a clear and specific decree that was issued from his throne and his position, and therefore could not be disputed.

The historian Josephus writes the following, "But let no one blame me for writing down every thing of this nature, as I find it in our ancient books; for as to that matter, I have plainly assured those that think me defective in any such point, or complain of my management, and have told them in the beginning of this history, that I intended to do no more than translate the Hebrew books into the Greek language, and promised them to explain those facts, without adding any thing to them of my own, or taking any thing away from them."[22]

Through this disclaimer we see that Josephus clearly reported what was recorded in the Hebrew Scripture, and what was viable and accurate historic records; and translated them into the Greek language, without any prejudice or opinion or change.

THE KING'S TROUBLING DREAM

Nebuchadnezzar was troubled by visions of a dream and called for his head magician, Daniel, to reveal the secret. Daniel chapter four records, *"Therefore made I a decree to bring in all the wise men of Babylon before me, that they might make known unto me the interpretation of the dream. Then came in the magicians, the astrologers, the Chaldeans, and the soothsayers: and I told the dream before them; but they did not make known unto me the interpretation thereof. But at the last Daniel came in before me, whose name was Belteshazzar, according to the name of my God, and in whom is the spirit of the holy gods: and before him I told the dream, saying, O Belteshazzar, master of the magicians, because I know that the spirit of the holy gods is in thee, and no secret troubleth thee, tell me the visions of my dream that I have seen, and the interpretation thereof."*[23] The Holy Spirit was the Spirit of God in Daniel. The heathen king acknowledged the supernatural help of Daniel's God. The words used here by the king regarding God were *Elohim.* It is a plural noun equivalent to the Hebrew *Elohim.*

Notice that Daniel was recognized as overseer of all the other master magicians. Daniel was regarded as being greater than all the learned men and religious devotees of his day. Daniel was not a magician or enchanter; his gift came directly from *Jehovah Elohim.* He was captive in Babylon even though he had been made a ruler. Daniel and his companions had *proved* their God and were made men of position; however, that position could be devastatingly ripped from them at any whim of Nebuchadnezzar. *Jehovah Elohim* was not slack regarding His promises. He had set *watchers* over the king; *watchers* are Holy Angels of God.

The other magicians were no doubt followers of *Zoroaster,* founder of the ancient Persian religion; and the wisdom of the Magi, who were originally a median tribe and were invested early with priestly rites. They guarded the sacred fire, recited hymns at dawn, and offered sacrifices. They had a reputation for magic arts, studied astrology, astronomy, and claimed to be able to do many things beyond human power, according to Dake.[24]

Nebuchadnezzar shares this vision: *"I saw in the visions of my head upon my bed, and, behold, a watcher and an holy one came down from heaven; He cried aloud, and said thus, Hew down the tree, and cut off his branches, shake off his leaves, and scatter his fruit: let the beasts get away from under it, and the fowls from his branches:Nevertheless leave the stump of his roots in the earth, even with a band of iron and brass, in the tender grass of the field; and let it be wet with the dew of heaven, and let his portion be with the beasts in the grass of the earth:Let his heart be changed from man's, and let a beast's heart be given unto him; and let seven times pass over him. This matter is by the decree of the watchers, and the demand by the*

word of the holy ones: to the intent that the living may know that the most High ruleth in the kingdom of men, and giveth it to whomsoever he will, and setteth up over it the basest of men."[25] This dream came from a Holy Angel from Heaven at the command of *watchers* and *holy ones,* carrying out the will of the Most High. These *watchers* are reported to oversee the affairs of men to enable them to bring about the will of God on earth.

Daniel interpreted the dream, by the Spirit of God, saying that the king will be driven from his dwelling to eat grass like the ox, to be wet with the dew of heaven, and that seven years will pass until he knows that the Most High rules.[26]

This matter was declared as a *decree by the holy watcher of God.* Daniel proceeded to give Nebuchadnezzar God's counsel; he advised the king to break off his sin and to show mercy on the poor that it may be lengthening of his tranquility. Daniel advised the king that if he would humble himself that this *curse* could be averted. According to the dream, this tree– its fruit and influence, its power, its reputation and its visibility– had reached the entire earth. As we have already referenced, antiquity acknowledges the feats and the accomplishments of this godlike king as exceeding the great accomplishment of *Hercules,* according to Josephus. At this height of rulership, Babylon and Nebuchadnezzar were *"one."*[27]

The Zoroastrian symbol of Ahura Mazda, known as the Faravahar. It was adapted by the Zoroastrians from the ancient symbol of the winged, horned sun disc.

Bel was recognized to be the source of this superpower, and Babylon was one of the wonders of the world. The walls were impressive, the hanging gardens were magnificent, the houses were built with precision. The beauty and the wealth of Babylon was splendid and compared to no other in superabundance.

One year later, after God had graced him with a twelve month period to correct his ways, the king looked upon his palace and his kingdom and said, *"Is not this great Babylon, that I have built for the house of the kingdom by the might of my power, and for the honour of my majesty?"*[28]

The king's words gained this response, as recorded in the book of Daniel: *"While the word was in the king's mouth, there fell a voice from heaven, saying, O king Nebuchadnezzar, to thee it is spoken; The kingdom is departed from thee. And they shall drive thee from men, and thy dwelling shall be with the beasts of the field: they shall make thee to eat grass as oxen, and seven times shall pass over thee, until thou know that the most High ruleth in the kingdom of men, and giveth it to whomsoever he will."*[29]

It is obvious that this voice from heaven was in response to a judgment that king Nebuchadnezzar deserved. He had been influenced by the false *gods* that ruled in Babylon to attribute his kingdom to *Bel* and not remember Daniel and the Lord. Nebuchadnezzar was lifted up in his own pride, and the pride of the Babylonian *gods*. In this kingdom as in many others before, the king and the *god* that empowered him became *"one."* Nebuchadnezzar dropped on all fours and was driven into the fields possessed to resemble the very *bull god* that he worshipped. The king, his *gods,* and his kingdom are one, because the *word* of that king was law, and his religion was law.

There is a disease called *Boanthropy:* a psychological disorder which causes a human to think and act like a bull. The king was driven from men and ate grass as the ox. His body was wet with the dew of heaven. His hair grew like the hair of an eagle and his nails became like birds claws. We found the disease *Boanthropy* in the nineteen hundred and thirty-three version of the *Shorter Oxford English Dictionary on Historical Principles*.

The images on the gates and walls of Babylon represented the *god* of Nebuchadnezzar. They are the body of a bull and the head of the king. He was ascribed by historians as one of the greatest monarchs who ever lived. The Babylon of that time period is esteemed by the world as *"a wonder."*

We have seen through our study men and women who *became* what they worshipped. *Bel Merodach* at the top of Babel is in the image of a *bull.* Great minds, great sovereigns, and even greater empires have fallen because of the worship of idols. We are speaking of the dark prince. He has taken possession of many names and companion images to shroud himself behind distorted myth and antiquities. Nebuchadnezzar became possessed with this *bull god,* and after seven years of behaving as one, he finally gave glory to *Jehovah Elohim* and was set free.

The Scripture describes it as this, *"And at the end of the days I Nebuchadnezzar lifted up mine eyes unto heaven, and mine understanding returned unto me, and I blessed the most High, and I praised and honoured him that liveth for ever, whose dominion is an everlasting dominion, and his kingdom is from generation to generation: And all the inhabitants of the earth are reputed as nothing: and he doeth according to his will in the army of heaven, and among the inhabitants of the earth: and none can stay his hand, or say unto him, What doest thou?"[30]*

XII

BABYLONIA FROM ANTIQUITY

In the scope of our examination and study of ancient Babylonia, we will look at certain cities, as well as, what we will call, *the greater ancient Babylonian plain.* It is a fascinating study to discover the custom, religion, accomplishments, lifestyles, mindsets and advanced knowledge spanning as far back as five thousand years.

Erech, the ancient city founded by Nimrod, sometimes known as *Uruk* or *Warka,* presents a phenomenal achievement of building ability. This city housed the royal residence of the hero king *Gilgamish* of Babylonia. *Erech* was a highly fortified city whose hero ruler's accomplishments were viewed as *mighty* and *godlike* by his people. Gilgamish, known as one of the earliest heroes, lived very near to the time of the flood of Noah.[1]

Excavations in these regions of Babylonia began in 1852. Early finds unearthed 50 foot high brick walls encircling the city and the beautifully ornamented mosaic parathion temple which included a number of pyramidal ziggurats. Thousands of Neo-Babylonian tablets were found, some of which were clay envelopes. Later excavations penetrated down, confirming chronology to nearly 4000 B.C. and unearthing the remains of a wall dating back to 3000 B.C.[2]

It is fascinating, however, to know that over five hundred tablets written in the very ancient form of "pictograph writing" confirmed the religious beliefs of ancient Babylonia. Our study shows only two deities, of which one preceded the other: the first being the *eternal self existent God,* and the other being the *fallen prince of this world.*[3]

Nineveh was famous for being the capital of the ancient Assyrian

Empire. Nineveh was three hundred miles north of Babylon. This ancient region, rich with similarities of rule and religion, must be included in our consideration of the greater Babylonian plain. Situated across the river *Tigris* on the eastern bank, the ancient Nineveh would later become known as the *"robber city"* overrunning other countries to enrich itself. With its ancient and colorful history, a wealth of treasures would begin to be discovered during the 1853 excavations. The great Assyrian king, *Ashurbanipal's* palace, was uncovered there; and the beautiful bas-relief, that depicted the King, standing in a chariot, about to start on a hunting expedition. Hunting of wild animals for sport was the practice of the heroes throughout that period in antiquity. His attendants were handing him the necessary weapons for the chase. Two high vaulted rooms were also uncovered, stacked high with priceless tablets. These large clay tablets were part of his royal library. The pursuit of knowledge and learning—mastery and perfection—has proven to be a major driving force of these ancient peoples. This great king must have been taught to read and write in various languages as one of

An impression of the god-king Gilgamesh, flanked by two manheadedm, winged beings, subduing two lions.

his inscriptions read, "I, Ashur-Bani-Pal, within the palace, learned the wisdom of *Nebu*... the entire art of writing on clay tablets. I made myself master of the various kinds of writing .... I read the beautiful clay tablets from Sumer and the Acadian writing, which is hard to master. I had the joy of reading inscriptions on stone before the time before the flood."[4]

This Prince's scholarly pursuit included literature, the study of the scribes, and an insatiable desire for enlightenment. He sent scribes throughout the regions of the Ancient Babylonian plane (Ashur, Babylon, Cuthah, Nippor, Akkad, Erech). He collected and copied clay books of astrology, history, grammar, geography, literature, law, and medicine, with letters, poems, oracles, incantations, chronicles and much more.

His library contained somewhere near *one hundred thousand* copies, making it one of the most valuable in antiquity. Great gallery rooms where the library was found contained a picture gallery—*this was only a small portion of this brilliant monarch's royal palace.* Interestingly, a later find in Nineveh corresponds with this find; it was another portion of a tablet completing the Chaldeans account of the *Deluge.* Later the Creation tablets were also found and published under the title the, *The Chaldean Account of Genesis.* Many resemblances of the biblical accounts of the flood were duplicated; constituting to many scholars' witness to dispute that such a disaster did happen.[5]

A large collection of ancient cuneiform tablets. Included among them is the "Epic of Gilgamesh," one of the oldest written works known to man. It details the supposedly divine origins and amazing strength of Gilgamesh.

This Assyrian king was a contender for mastery of learning. Their science, religion, culture, warfare, and consistent willingness to contest for greater mastery of these areas, presented us with a complete concept of the mindsets of these rulers. This wealth of knowledge was handed down from the earliest post-deluvian generations.

From this ancient greater Babylonian plain and the region of Armenia we locate the earliest civilizations in possession of advanced knowledge. Before the formation of the old dynasties and empires, the inhabitants of that region were in possession of information transferred to them and recorded in their history. The mindset of those who would be accredited with princely titles such as *giants, god-kings, heroes, mighty men* and *mighty hunters,* exceeded their physical strengths, making them seem superhuman. The path to becoming a prince was becoming the by-product of their constant pursuit of learning and embracing the religion and the sciences of the day. The driving force behind their ambitions to rule would lead some to migrate from this fertile great Babylonian plain, and would leave an unmistakable mark in history, undoubtedly affecting societies to come.

Hunting lions was the preferred sport of Assyrian royalty. The king most known for this dangerous sport was Ashurbanipal.

Pezron, who wrote *The Antiquities of Nations* particular to Celtae or Gauls, records what I believe to be a great wealth of historical, chronological, and etymological discoveries. These discoveries are consistent with the records of Scripture we will view regarding Canaan, and they are unknown to the proponents of Greek and Romans mythology. I believe that Pezron, a Doctor in Divinity, as well as the wealth of historians in agreement with the Holy Scriptures, help to verify the biblical cannon and its validity both in the Old and the New Covenants.

Pezron traces the posterity of *Gomer*, in agreement with Josephus, and as recorded in the tenth chapter of Genesis; documenting historically many of their accomplishments and achievements as titan giant which predated the time of Abraham. This migration, as recorded by Pezron's antiquity, is as follows: *"For you must know, that in the first age of the Postdiluvian World, several of the Chaldeans retired into the Mountains of Armenia. There the more easily to contemplate the stars, and to live with the more safely from the invasions of other people. Auguries, Divinations, Magick, and Enchantments, were then much in use among most Nations of the World; and they undertook nothing of any considerable Importance, without consulting their Diviners, and the like: Its well known that the Chaldeans in those Times were looked upon to be the greatest Masters , in these Over-curious and Diabolical Sciences.*

The sacae, who were their Neighbours were not wanting to become Disciples, and were, if I may so say, initiated by them into all those Mysteries of Superstition and Iniquity. It was therefore in the Chaldean Schools, that they chiefly learnt all that which was most Refined and Secret in those

Hunting lions was considered an excellent way to show one immense strength and skill. Adult male lions, often exceeding 550 pounds in weight and 8 feet in length from nose to rear, can often reach upwards of 10 feet in height when standing upright on their back legs.

Prophane and Dangerous Arts. Hence it was that they learned to take their nearest Relations even their own Sisters to be their Wives, and to make this Criminal, not to say, Abominable and Incestuous Alliance, a Point of Honour and Religion also: And it was from the same Principles of this dangerous Doctrine, that some Ages after the Sacick or Titan Princes, I mean Uranus, Saturn, and Jupiter, Married their own Sisters: It was fro hence they learnt, as I may say to stimatize their Bodies, that is to imprint certain Figures, Marks, or Characters upon them, whereby they were Consecrated, not to the Service of their Imaginary Deities, but to the worship of Devils, and the Prince of Darkness, that seduced them: Lastly to pass over many other Particulars, it was in this School that they learnt to inspect the Entrails of Beasts, and perhaps of Men too, in order to have their more Important Divinations, the more confirmed by the Fibres or Lobes of the Liver; This the Grecians in their Language called Jecur Inspiscere, or Jecur Consulere, that is, to consult, or rather by way of Divination to inspect the Liver; It's so certain that these Sorts of Divinations came from the Chaldeans, that the Famous Nabuchadonosor (Nebuchadnezzar), King of Chaldea and Babylon, made a Use of it before he laid siege to Jerusalem. For being come to the Meeting of Two Ways, One of which led to Judaea, and the other to the Country Ammon, and not knowing which Way he should go; the Scripture says, that beside other Divinations, he consulted the Liver of Beasts, (Eze 21:21) and there upon without any more ado determined to go to Judaea, in order to destroy Jerusalem to which he believed his Gods had directed him."[6]

An ancient skull that has been trepanned, a medical procedure in which a hole is drilled in the skull. The bone growth and regeneration show that the patient survived this brain surgery over 5,000 years ago.

Continuing with Pezron, it is clear that he addresses a time in history that sheds tremendous light on the activities of these titan giants–specifically during the time of Abraham. He factually acknowledges that these titans exceeded others in

A ceremonial bronze age razor used for religious rituals and sacrifices.

strength and bulk of body, and ruled over all the earth.[7] The prophet Isaiah informs us also that these giants were ancient masters of the world, and that they drove kings of nations from their thrones.[8] (Later we will address Isaiah chapter fourteen: Babylon and Nebuchadnezzar). Quoting Pezron, *"The Titans thererfore were not a fabulous and imaginary Race of Men, tho' the Greeks disguised the history of them with fables; but they were a potent people and great Soldiers, descended from the Giants, who made so much Noise all the World over.*

Besides all this we are to add, that they were much addicted Magic, Auguries, Divinations, Satanical Delusions and Inchantments; the greatest Persons among them, viz. the Priests Sacrificers, Kings themselves, and Princes of the Blood, were the most of any inclined to these Prophane and Diabolical Curiosities. Then it was that the Devil, who is called the Prince of the World, seduced almost the whole Earth, keeping the Hearts and Minds of Men and Bondage. This wretched Dominion lasted too long, and was not destroy'd but by the Power and Cross of Christ. Hence one of the Fathers of the Church, (Euseb. perp. 1.2.c:5.) who had narrowly inspected into these Things, had reason to say, that in these unhappy Times they placed Giants, Tyrants, Magicians, and Enchanters in the Number of their Kings, and afterwards of their Gods."[9]

JOSEPHUS CONCERNING ALEXANDER THE GREAT

Now Alexander when he had taken Gaza, made haste to go up to Jerusalem; and Jaddua the high priest, when he heard that, was in an agony, and under terror, as not knowing how he should meet the Macedonians, since the king was displeased at his foregoing disobedience. He therefore ordained that the people should make supplications, and should join with him in offering sacrifices to God, whom he sought to protect that nation, and to deliver them from the perils that were coming upon them; whereupon God warned him in a dream, which came upon him after he had offered sacrifice, that he should take courage, and adorn the city, and open the gates; that the rest should appear in white garments, but that he and the priests should meet Alexander in the habits proper to their order, without the dread of any ill consequences, which the providence of God would prevent. Upon which, when he rose from his sleep, he greatly rejoiced; and declared to all the warning he had received from God. According to which the dream he acted entirely, and so waited for the coming of Alexander the Great.

And when he understood that he was not far from the city, he went out in procession with the priests, and the multitude of citizens, the procession was venerable and the manner of it different from that of other nations. It reached to a place called Sapha; which name, translated into Greek, signifies 'a prospect', for you have thence a prospect both of Jerusalem and of the temple; and when the Phoenicians and the Chaldeans that followed him, thought they should have the liberty to plunder the city, and torment the high priests to death, which the king's displeasure fairly promised them, the very reverse of it happened; Alexander,

Alexander sought supernatural help from many gods. He is shown here with the horns of Amun, the Egyptian sun god.

"Alexander the Great in the Temple of Jerusalem," Sebastiano Conca

when he saw the multitude at a distance, in white garments, while the priests stood clothed with fine linen, and the high priest in purple and scarlet clothing, with his mitre on his head, having the golden plate whereon the 'name of God' was engraved, he approached by himself, and adored that name, and first saluted the high priest, The Jews also did all together with one voice, salute Alexander, and encompass him about; whereupon the kings of Syria and the rest were surprised at what Alexander had done, and supposed him disordered in his mind. However, Parmenio alone went up to him, and asked him how it came to pass that, when all others him, he should adore the high priest of the Jews? To whom he replied, "I did not adore him, but that God who hath honored him with his high priesthood; for I saw this very person in a dream, in this very habit, when I was at Dios in Macedonia, who, when I was considering with myself how I might obtain the dominion of Asia, exhorted me to make no delay, but boldly to pass over the sea thither, for that he would conduct my army, and would give me dominion over the Persians; whence it is, that having seen no other in that habit, and now seeing this person in it, and remembering that vision, and the exhortation which I had in my dream, I believe that I bring this army under the divine conduct, and destroy the power of the Persians, and that all things according to what is in my own mind.

Alexander offered sacrifices to God, according to the high priests direction. And when the book of Daniel was shown him, wherein Daniel declared that one of the Greeks, would destroy the empire of Persia, Alexander was glad and knew it was him.

—Flavius Josephus[10]

ozrah.
habited , nei-
com genera-
r shall the A-
ther shal the
d there.

of the desert
houses shalbe
and ||owles
hatyres shall

tes of the I-
olate houses,
ant palaces :
me , and her
ed.

III.

of Israel. 4
n ouer Babel.
syria. 29 Pa-

k O wil haue
cob, and wil
rael, and set
owne land :
gers shalbe
y shal cleaue

l take them,
ace : and the
esse them in
for seruants
y shall take
ptiues they
uer their op-
passe in the

---

vp against vs.

9 ‖ Hell from beneath is mooued for thee to meet thee at thy comming : it stir-reth vp the dead for thee, euen all the †chiefe ones of the earth ; it hath raised vp from their thrones, all the kings of the nations.

10 All they shall speake and say vnto thee ; Art thou also become weake as we : art thou become like vnto vs ?

11 Thy pompe is brought downe to the graue , and the noyse of thy violes : the worme is spread vnder thee, and the wormes couer thee.

12 How art thou fallen from heauen, ‖O Lucifer, sonne of the morning ? how art thou cut downe to the ground, which didst weaken the nations ?

13 For thou hast said in thine heart, I wil ascend into heauen, I wil exalt my throne aboue the starres of God : I wil sit also vpon the mount of the con-gregation, in the sides of the North.

14 I wil ascend aboue the heights of the cloudes, I wil bee like the most High.

15 Yet thou shalt be brought downe to hel, to the sides of the pit.

16 They that see thee shal narrowly looke vpon thee, and consider thee, say-ing ; Is this the man that made the earth to tremble, that did shake kingdomes ?

17 That made the world as a wil-dernesse, and destroyed the cities there-of ‖ that opened not the house of his pri-soners ?

18 All the kings of the nations, euen all of them lie in glory, euery one in his owne house.

THE TAUNT

Considered by many to be the mightiest metropolis of the ancient world, Babylon was built to the credit of Hammurabi (1728-1686 B.C.); however, the great Nebuchadnezzar (604-562 B.C.) took it to another level. According to the *Antiquities of the Jews* by Josephus, Nebuchadnezzar erected elevated places for walking of stone, and made them to resemble mountains. He also planted many sorts of trees. His magnificent pensile paradise built for his comfort, and his wife, was considered a wonder of Babylon. The expansion, refinement, and perfection of this empire reached its height under the rule of Nebuchadnezzar (604-562 B.C.).[1]

To confirm reports of antiquity and the magnificence and authenticity of this empire, careful excavation work began dating from 1899 through 1913, providing information about the phrase *Babylon The Great.* The discoveries were no less than fantastic, confirming the *Ziggurat* and the *Hanging Gardens.* In addition, a wall was found surrounding the main city that was more than 14 miles long and 136.5 feet thick. Many city gates were excavated. One famous gate displayed 575 enameled dragons, bulls, and lions.

The north entrance called the processional street passing under the *Ishtar Gate* went past the royal palace. The Temple of *Marduk,* meaning *the creator and king of the universe,* was also unearthed. The palace of the king was gorgeously decorated with a magnificent banquet hall and throne room which was 56 feet wide and 168 feet long. The *E-Temen-an-Ki,* or the *house of the foundation platform of heaven and earth,* was believed to have been the ruins of the ill-fated *Tower of Babel.*

OPPOSITE
*1611 King James,
Isaiah 14:9-18.*

The *Hanging Gardens* were found on the extensive ruins of a quadrangle area. This quadrangle area was comprised of high-vaulted crypts and subterranean cellar rooms. These extensive ruins are believed to be the foundation structure of the famous gardens, one of the *Seven Wonders of the Ancient World.* The place for the distribution of oil and barley to workers of the nation was also found.[2] One must immediately recognize that when speaking of Babylon, Nebuchadnezzar immediately comes to mind. No doubt his world wide reputation of being a feared, tyrannical, ambitious ruler has caused this synonymous affiliation.

"The Hanging Gardens of Babylon" Maartin Heeskerck

The major prophet *Isaiah* is the single most quoted Messianic prophet. His ministry as a prophet of the Lord involved judgements over nations, prophetic promises to the nation of Israel, predictions of the life and ministry of Christ, as well as, accurate prophetic provisions for the church. Isaiah received his call in the year King Uziah died. He saw the exalted Lord by vision, receiving the consecration from the Lord to his lips and accepting the commission as a prophet of the Lord. (see Isa. 6:1-8).

OPPOSITE

A kudurru "boundary marker" found in Susa. It features the most prominent gods in Babylonian/Susan pantheon. At the bottom of the marker is the horned serpent, a symbol of Merodach, also called Marduk.

Declaring the end from the beginning, speaking of things to come, calling things to be, raising up and pulling down, building or destroying; these are known to be within the nature and the ability of the true *Lord of the Universe.* With reference to Babylon and the captive people, Israel, the Lord promises to have mercy on Jacob; and declares His choosing of Israel, their liberation from Babylon, their deliverance from their oppressors, their return to the *Promise Land,* and the rest from their sorrows (see Isa. 14:1-3). As a true prophet of God, Isaiah receives assignment from *Jehovah Elohim* to declare a prophetic taunt against Babylon and its proud, pompous, titan tyrant king. This word, predictive in nature, preceded the magnificence that Babylon would reach. Isaiah foresaw the pride and rebellion of its future monarch and released the most accurate definition of its downfall. Knowing that the invisible dark forces would be simultaneously addressed in this taunt of prophetic judgement, we are directed at this time to deal firstly with the natural fulfillment of God's powerful predictive word.

The prophet is inspired and commanded by the divine Spirit to foretell as a proverb to *Babylon* and *Nebuchadnezzar* that judgment is imminent. In the year 1611, the King James Bible renders verse four, *"proverb against the king of Babylon;"* with a side margin note calling it *"a taunting speech." "Then shalt thou use this mockage upon the king of Babylon,"* found in the Bishops' first edition, in the year 1568. The word is rendered again as a *proverb, a jeer, a song of derision, a taunt-song, a taunt over the king,* and finally *a parable, or poem.*

The all knowing, foreseeing, omnipotence of God would be released through His prophet as a *taunt and derision* recorded to reveal the specificity of God's description involving future events. Isaiah is directed in verse four to predict in proverb, foretell in taunting speech, declare in poem, predict in parable; to prophetically taunt a future king, to release a taunt-song against the height of a future kingdom, to sing a

specific song of derision, to jeer at the king of Babylon, and to use a mockage, as he is inspired by the Spirit of the Lord, declaring in speech what is yet to come to pass.

This reveals the power of God's word–His ability to release the answers and His specific intentions, given against the wicked, in a word, *even through a human vessel.* The Lord enables His prophets to see; inspires His prophets to speak; and empowers His prophet to know. The Lord used Isaiah to address the spiritual forces of darkness–the so called *gods* of Babylon–as well as, give the description of its fall from the height of its future pomp, and finally the death and judgement of Nebuchadnezzar.

He speaks of the oppressor ceasing and of the golden city. He speaks of the power of the wicked being broken and the scepter of rule being no more. The prophecy goes further, stating that rest will come to the people and singing will break forth, after the smiter whose anger and continual striking is no more. He sings of the freedom of the region and predicts the liberation of Creation.

Then in verse nine, he speaks of *Sheol* or the nether parts of the earth being moved. A good rendering would be *'stirred'*–specifically at the death of this titan king. For the prophetic taunt song continues, stating that Sheol stirs up the dead for the king; clearly speaking of *Rephaim* or *giants*–the chief ones of the earth. The side note in the 1611 King James Bible says *"or great goats,"* defining these giants. These titans who lived, died, and drove kings from their thrones; who were then dethroned from their own reign, are stirred to meet this king at his coming, as we previously mentioned in Pezron.

OPPOSITE
A close-up of the kudurru stone shows not only the star of Ishtar but also the crescent and star, a symbol that continues to be used by numerous factions, nations and religions.

Seen here is the star of Ishtar, the moon of Sin and the sun of Shamash. These symbols have been used by many peoples over many millennia and given many names, but always represent the same spirit.

This prophetic mockage continues, in divine accuracy, describing the future conversations that will take place in the nether parts; as ancient titan *god-kings,* together with contemporary warriors–*Rephaims, giants,* or *great goats*–begin to jeer with their own mocking conversation, at the destruction and judgment of this so-called god-king, Nebuchadnezzar. They jeer at the elimination of his pomp, and his transformation into their shared weak and defeated condition, imprisoned in Sheol.

"The Prophet Isaiah,"
Raphael

Isaiah continues his jeer against the assumed titles ascribed to this king and kingdom. They are systematically addressed with taunt and prophetic prediction: *"light bringer...day star...son of the morning...shining one...son of the dawn?"*[3] Isaiah follows with predictive judgement: *"blasphemous satanic king of Babylon...what a fall from heaven on high...how low and limp you lie.....sprawling helpless across the nations."*[4]

The prophet continues revealing the ambition, the pomp, and the presumption, of the king of Babylon as the cause of his judgement. The earlier translations better render the words, *"I will ascend"* in Isaiah chapter fourteen verses thirteen and fourteen as *"I will climb."* The prophet foretells of this king's decision to etch his position in history by being like the *Most High. Isaiah* continues, *"Yet you will be brought down to hell to the sides of the pit;"* you will be looked upon and considered. The tone of this mockage is clear in identifying his termination in hell. This prophetic mockage continues again to describe the imprisonment of the tyrant with others that shared his same persuasion. This spirit that has operated from the dawn of time propagating the life, religion, motivations, and cruelties of this titan race, drove them to aggressive self-seeking, possession coveting, and oppression against the human race. This prophecy is subject to what I call *"the law of double fulfillment."* We will address the fall of Satan in a later chapter.

SAINT JEROME AND BISHOP LUCIFER

Bishop Lucifer of Cagliari first appears in history as an envoy from Liberius of Rome to the Emperor of Constantius the second, requesting the convening of the church council. At the council of Milan in A.D. 355 he defended Athanasius of Alexandria against Arian attempts to secure his condemnation by Western Bishops. It was reported that Constatius the second, a supporter of Arian theology confined Bishop Lucifer for three days in the palace, where Bishop Lucifer continued to argue vehemently. Along with Eusebius of Vercelli and Dionysus of Milan, he was exiled. He traveled first to Syria, then to Palestine and finally to Thebes in Egypt. In exile he wrote fiery pamplets to the emperor in which he proclaimed himself to be ready to suffer martyrdom for his beliefs.

Saint Jerome was one of the most important Church Fathers and Bible scholars of early Christianity. Following a vision in A.D. 374., he changed his life to devote himself to the study of the Bible. He was ordained a priest in A.D. 379 and was commissioned by Pope Damascus. After Pope Damascus's death this work was completed and Saint Jerome left Rome and established a monastery in Bethlehem where he lived the rest of his life.

Jerome's translation of the Old Testament was revolutionary; he created his translation directly from the Hebrew and Syriac and his New Testament translation directly from the Greek. The result became known as the "Vulgate" and became the only standard and only translation sanctioned by the Roman Catholic Church.

All other translations of the Bible were outlawed by the "new" Pope and Saint Jerome's Latin Vulgate was the only Bible that was allowed to be read. There is no evidence that Saint Jerome was at all involved in outlawing other translations of the Bible. He seemed more a scholar than a political leader; unfortunately, all other languages and translations of the Bible were deemed illegal. Enter hundreds of years of a period in time accurately named, "The Dark Ages."

Catholic Bishop who died in A.D. 371 He was a bishop of Cagliare in Sardina known for his opposition to Arianism. He was venerated as a Saint in Sardinia, thou his status remains controversial.

"Saint Jerome in His Study"
by Domenico Ghirlandaio

Saint Lucifer formed a small sect called the Luciferians. A chapel in Cagliari's cathedral is dedicated to Saint Lucifer. Marie Josephine Louise of Savoy, wife of Louis XV111 of France, is buried there.

The Church of Cagliari celebrated the feast of Saint Lucifer on the 20th of May. Two Archbishops of Sardina wrote for and against the sanctity of Bishop Lucifer. The Congregation of the Inquistion imposed silence on both parties, and decreed that the veneration of Saint Lucifer should stand as it was. Saint Jerome contended with Saint Lucifer and his Luciferians. Jerome considered Saint Lucifer to be the author of the schism, which was splitting the church at that time.

When it came time for Saint Jerome to translate Isaiah chapter fourteen he translated verse nineteen as the Latin word "lucifer" which was used as an adjective. The use of the word lucifer, meaning "light bringer" was a fine translation from the Hebrew texts. According to the Catholic encyclopedia, the name lucifer originally denotes the planet Venus, emphasizing its brilliance. Venus is the last planet we see before the sun dawns; it ushers in the morning light.

The Vulgate employs the word "light of the morning." Metaphorically, the word is applied to the King of Babylon in Isaiah as preeminent among the princes of his time.

In Christian tradition this meaning of lucifer as a proper name has prevailed; but the Church Fathers maintain that Lucifer is not the proper name of the devil, but denotes only the state from which he has fallen. By some translators capitalizing the Latin word lucifer in Isaiah Chapter fourteen verse nineteen, it was adopted over time, after the poets used it, as the proper name of the devil. In poetry (is) was used in the sentence, "As proud as Lucifer," and that terminology caught on.

This hiding behind false names and images has been a strategy of the prince of darkness since the beginnings of time. He is not the day star. He is not the light of the morning. He is not the son of righteousness. He is not God's Son. He is not the sun god. The devil is not given a "proper" name in the Bible but he has been given 33 adjectives by Jehovah Elohim.[5]

"Saint Jerome" depicted by Michelangelo Merisi da Caravaggio

GIANT CITIES OF BASHAN

We will discover in this most ancient region of the world, a kingdom completely forgotten. Though its name is no longer spoken, we will find, through a historical journey, rich beginnings, territorial dominions, age old alliances, and an appointment for Messiah's complete victory. *Bashan* is a fruitful, distinct, region on the east of Jordan referred to as *"Land of Bashan."* It extends from the border of Gilead on the South, and *Hermon* on the North; and from the *Arabah* or *Jordan Valley* on the West, to *Salshah* of the *Geshurites* on the East.

 Bashan was called the land of *"sacred romance,"* visited and occupied again from the earliest days after the flood. Thousands of years ago this region was recognized, as its name implies, by the union of *fallen angels* with the *daughters of men*. Called also the *"Land of the Giants,"* all of Bashan was occupied by giants in ancient times. Many remains which still existed as late as several centuries ago, were discovered by travelers, who described houses built of huge blocks; made of dark marble; with stone doors, windows, staircases, and galleries. The roofs and the rest of the buildings were also made of stone blocks. These houses show evidence of their giant inhabitants: their walls varying from 5 to 8 feet in thickness, and their roofs as thick as 6 inches; with ceiling heights reaching 20 to 30 feet; and doors higher than ten feet. Bible records are full of descriptions of the local scenes and terrain of that land. The graphic descriptions and historic records found in the Word of God, and confirmed by historians, shed an amazing light on the religion, the culture, the struggles, and most importantly, the victory of Christ our *Messiah*. From the remotest historic period, strange mysteries

OPPOSITE
Ruins in Bashan, located near the Sea of Galilee, thought to be the location in which Jesus removed the demons from the demoniac of Gadara.

have been connected with that kingdom. The *Rephaim,* or giants, have been known to fortify there. Descriptions of the strength of its oaks (Ezek. 27:6), the beauty of its mountain scenery, the unrivaled luxuriance, the fertility of its plains makes us to know that *Bashan* was regarded as almost an earthly paradise. Remnants of the oak forests still clothe the mountain sides. Its cattle was made up of the fiercest, most powerful bulls of Bashan.[1]

United under the rulership of *Og* the giant, the region boasted sixty fortified cities–walled, fenced, and barred. Although its name has disappeared from geographical history, yet the definitive description of its boundaries are clearly defined in the Holy Scriptures.[2] Interestingly, *Bashan* was also used throughout history as a place of refuge because of the availability of its rocky terrain. It was said that if someone could arrive to Bashan, that they may never be found.[3]

This entire kingdom was steeped in the worship of *Ashteroth-Karnaim,* the horned goddess of fertility, and *Baal,* the horned god called *Elion* by many giant tribes. The capital city and stronghold of the *Rephaim* was *Ashteroth-Karnaim,* named after their mysterious *"two-horned Astarte."* The discoveries of houses, deserted halls, massive ruins, and sculptured images of their crescent moon were verified to have withstood for forty centuries. The rich plains, and wooded hills, offered a tempting prospect to many would-be invaders: however, Og, the giant king of *Bashan,* was an exceptional specimen, with strength and obstinate determination. This giant whose bedstead was made of iron and measured 18.5 feet in length and was 8 feet and 4 inches wide, possessed a potent genealogy directly linked to the father of the *Rephaim.* This king was acknowledged for his supremacy as a warrior and was followed faithfully by the inhabitants of his kingdom, who were also of the giant tribes.[4]

Og and his army came out with determination and full fury against Israel. Their battles were no doubt fierce, however, the Lord had spoken *"Fear him not: for I will deliver him, and all his people, and his land, into thy hand"* (Deut. 3:2). God delivered *Bashan* into the hands of Israel. *Og,* the giant, was killed along with all of the inhabitants of that land, and although there were many other giant tribes, it seemed that the Rephaim branch was almost extinct. Sixty walled cities and many unwalled villages and towns were taken. All the land along the River Jordan was taken–from the Dead Sea on the South, to Mt. Hermon on the North; all the cities of the plain, all of Gilead, and all of Bashan. (Deut. 3:1-11).

David the king, a warrior who overcame Goliath, was also a priest

OPPOSITE
A Phoenician idol of a horned goddess with a sun disc in her horns. It represents Astarte, Asherah and Ashtoreth.

The Temple of Obelisks at Byblos, built in honor of the "Lady of Byblos" in 1600 B.C. This "Lady of Byblos" is the same as Ashtoreth, Astarte and the other horned goddesses of the Canaanites.

and a prophet. His kingdom would be a type of a kingdom that will never end. Under the inspiration of the Spirit of God, the most astounding Messianic prophecies were uttered, with precise detail, demonstrating the ability of the only *God*, the true *God*, the one who says it and brings it to pass. No doubt in his fifth Messianic Psalm revealing the sufferings of Christ, David the prophet was speaking as he was moved by the Holy Ghost. The position of prophetic intercession enabled the spirit of priesthood–the spirit of Christ–to testify beforehand of His own sufferings. This inspired psalm spoke relevantly to what would take place during their time, as well as simultaneously spoke prophetically of the accomplishment of Christ's victory on behalf of all of mankind (Psalm 22). Recording beforehand the agony, lamentation and moaning or roaring of Christ's prayers to His Father during "His Passion." The Spirit describes clearly the antagonism, the laughter, the despising, and the scorn, that all men released against the suffering Savior. Reproach and derision was voiced throughout the mob that seemed to be, and certainly was, moved by the invisible forces of darkness. The prophetic word describes beforehand men's sayings and scorn, *"they shake the head, saying, He trusted on the LORD that he would deliver him: let him deliver him."*[5] In verse 15 the Spirit continues by describing His thirst; the presence of a human assembly of the wicked; and the accuracy of the crucifixion–"they pierced my hands and my feet." The stripes that He had taken had so wounded His flesh that His bones could be seen. His garments were parted among the soldiers; lots were cast upon His vesture. The Messiah continues in confidence, *"I will declare thy name unto my brethren: in the midst of the congregation will I praise thee...My praise shall be of thee in the great congregation: I will pay my vows before them that fear him. The meek shall eat and be satisfied: they shall praise the LORD that seek him"*[6] A prophetic supernatural conclusion is hundreds of years in advance, declaring that the kingdom is the *Lord's* and *He is the governor among the nations.* This seemingly helpless condition of the crucified Master is accompanied by a victorious herald. Declaring that a seed will serve Him, a generation will come, a people will rise up and declare His righteousness; and that the provision of *Salvation* is paid for. This is the clearest evidence of the omniscience and omnipotence of the Lord declaring to the smallest detail His sacrificial work to deliver

A 3,000 year old terra-cotta drinking vessel in the shape of a bull's head.

mankind; however, it is important for us to note the activities of the invisible spirit of darkness, and the presence of the demonic hoards, to oppose–hoping to see a defeat rather than a victory.

Psalm 22 verse 12 reads, *"Many bulls have compassed me: strong bulls of Bashan have beset me round."* He continues revealing that these *bulls* opened their mouths to devour Him like a ravening lion. Bulls are emblems of brutal strength: they gore and trample down. The bulls of Bashan were the largest and fiercest of all. *"Strong bulls of Bashan,"* acknowledged by Christ, no doubt speaks of the many invisible demon spirits territorially ruling through deception and oppression. These devils are the same spirits who would diabolically romanticize Bashan with the absurd title, *"Land of Sacred Romance";* and for thousands of years wage a campaign to stop the coming seed of the woman. Giant tribes consumed with their nature are proven to be their offspring. These were the propagators of their religion, *the religion of the titans,* marked by images of the horned bull *Baal* and the two-horned goddess *Ashteroth.*

Ironically, during His victorious earthly ministry, when the Master would teach the multitudes, it is said that He did so on the grassy slopes of Bashan's hills.[7] He miraculously fed the multitudes two times–*giving in the land of takers, providing in a land of consumers, loving in a land of haters.* These devils were, no doubt, infuriated further that He would take His close disciples on the boundary of Bashan's kingdom, and there reveal His glorious transformation on the top of *Mount Hermon.*[8] It is also no doubt that their encounter with Him on the western slopes while they were inhabiting the body of the demoniac of Gad-era, made the truth be known, responding to the Lord's question, *"What is your name?"* In fear and pride they retorted, *"My name Is Legion: for we are many,"* revealing their age old hold on that part of the world. They asked Him not to cast them out of the region. These *many* bulls of Bashan were unified by assignment in the life of the Gadarene. *"My name is Legion: for WE ARE MANY."*[9]

They were unified by assignment throughout the ages to spread the religion of the fallen angels, and now they were unified by assignment in Psalm 22. *Joshua,* the warrior of Israel had played a significant role of strength and courage. The Lord's covenant with Abraham and Israel to possess the land of promise and over throw the giants was entrusted into his hands. The name *Joshua* means *"savior."* The conquest of Canaan recorded in the book of Joshua consisted of his military invasion to overthrow and drive out the inhabitants of the land with the wisdom he received from Moses and the direction from God to "be of good courage."[10] His readiness to keep the book of the law in his heart and in his mouth and to meditate of its truth, and receive its light, would enable him to face the many *giant nations* of the land of Canaan, defeating them with the help of God. Joshua was an exceptional military general, trained by Moses himself, and yet the directions of God supplied him, and Israel, with the supernatural help needed to overcome insurmountable odds. The promise was already given; however, the possession of the land was necessary, and only possible by facing the many giant tribes and engaging them in continual battle. The children of Israel were warring against beings of abnormal bodily size before whom they seemed as grasshoppers. All the giants would be described by the Hebrew word

OPPOSITE
The Gilgal Refaim (The Circle of the Rephaim), located in the Land of Bashan. A massive monument, of unknown purpose, the Gilgal Rafaim was built over 5,000 years ago, utilizing over 37,000 tons of stone. This amazing site and the other roughly 8,500 megalithic sites in the Land of Bashan, to this day, have barely been studied, due to the difficulty of reaching them and the unrest in the region.

'gibbor,' translated *giant,* meaning powerful, mighty, or strong man. The nature of *nephil* meaning *bully* or *tyrant,* as well as *giant* and *mighty,* portrays the merciless cruelty of these nations. It seems significant that prior to the conquest of Canaan, the Lord would present Israel with the opportunity to slay the great king *Og* of *Bashan,* and virtually annihilate the *Rephaim.* It seems prophetical, the boastful title, *"Land of the Giants,"* and *"Land of Sacred Romance"*—titles that reveal clearly these giants' identification with their original fallen fathers. It is possible that they identified themselves and are recognized prophetically, as representing forerunners in living, behaving, worshipping, and spreading the religion of the titans. Pursuant to their virtual annihilation, Joshua and his army would face and defeat all the giant tribes, and by this, would accomplish the possession of the land of promise. David the king was also a type of Christ, whose kingdom destroyed the remaining giants that were a terror to Israel at the time.[11]

Jesus is our Savior, our Deliverer, His name means *"Jehovah has become our salvation."* In making reference to the demonic spirits

The Makthar megoliths, a set of solid stone burial chambers, similar to the massive stone houses that can be found in the Land of Bashan.

raging against Him, while He hung there on the cross, He identifies them as strong bulls of *Bashan*. The bulls of *Bashan* were known to be the most powerful, vicious, and destructive bulls; they were also the largest, and are now extinct. It is reasonable to conclude that the Lord identifies His enemies. These spirits united in rebellious assignment, at the cross, together with the imprisoned angels that left their first estate (2 Pet. 2:4). These angels that sinned, spreading the message of the abominable "sacred romance," are confined in Tartaros (a dark abyss; a place of punishment). These imprisoned angels did not keep their own realm but left enamored by the daughters of men (Jude 6,7). By addressing the presence of many *"bulls of Bashan,"* Christ, by the Holy Ghost, reveals the union of assignment, as well as the nature and the might, of these invisible demonic spirits of darkness. By naming them, *"strong bulls of Bashan,"* He identifies the *"bull like nature"* and describes the demonic destroyers that will stop at nothing in their continual rebellion in battling the Godhead and apposing mankind. Christ identifies these spirits with the mightiest bulls, associated with

The Lanyon Quoit, a large dolmen, like the ones in the Land of Bashan, located in the Cornwall, England. The capstone originally rested at 7 feet high and is 9 feet wide , 17.5 feet tall and weighs in at 27,000 pounds.

the *Rephaim's* rebellion and the *nephil* nature. Identifying these spirits at the cross as the most powerful devils ever gathered in one place, at one time. It is reasonable to conclude, with complete assurance, that the prince of darkness (satan), had gathered with his mightiest generals and his lewdest leading dignitaries, rulers, and spiritual wickedness; releasing the most murderous devilish influence, to witness the death of the *Holy One.* The proponents of the profane religion of fertility, the two-horned, the crescent moon, of the titans, the tyrants, and the wicked of this world, are revealed to us clearly by Christ. Their presence in great numbers of fortification, to witness their so-called victory, was to their demise. They were being delivered into the Savior's hands. This is the great conquest of Calvary; this is the fall of the mighty, the paralysis of him who had the power of death–*that is the devil.* This is the greatest victory of the ages; the ransacking of the strongman's house; the spoiling of all of the powers of darkness (Col. 2:15). Christ stripped and put off the power that Satan had to condemn the human race. Christ triumphed, through the death of the cross. This is the conquest of Calvary–*"He shall bruise thy head"* (Gen 3:15). This was payment made in full; inheritance through giving (John 3:16); corruption conquered by Christ; rebellion defeated through obedience; and darkness overcome by the light (John 1:5). The

A giant stone house in the Land of Bashan.

The Land of Bashan in modern times has come to be known as the Golan Heights and continues to be a strategic military position in the region.

darkness could not siege upon, stop, detect, or overcome the true light of the world. The Word is light, the Word is with God, the Word is God. He said it and He performed it. He was put to death in the flesh then quickened by the Spirit–made alive spiritually. He then preached to the spirits in Tartarus (1 Pet. 3:18-19). In death, He was victorious. In resurrection, He is glorious; and as our High Priest He lives to make intercession for us.[12]

This great plan of God, His bright shining wisdom in a mystery, was in the heart of Jehovah before the world, to the profit for our glory (1 Cor. 2:7-8). None of the princes of this world could comprehend it, because light is foreign to darkness; had these demonic princes known it, they would not have crucified the Lord of Glory.[13]

WAR IN HEAVEN

The ministry of John the Beloved developed through a great love for Christ. He was called the disciple whom Jesus loved. Along with Peter and James, he had access, through invitation, to learn, to witness, and to see, some things that, no doubt, were God's choosing for him. The grace of his call would lead him to witness the resurrection of Jairus's daughter and the transfiguration of Christ on Mount Hermon. This grace would enable him to be entrusted with the care of Mary, the mother of the Lord, at the scene of the cross. He is a pillar among the original apostles–anointed to operate as an apostle and prophet. The Book of Revelation is meant to uncover, to lift a curtain, and to allow a clear look into things to come. The Greek word *apokalupsis,* translated revelation, means *"to reveal"* or *"to make clear."* He was commissioned to write what was revealed to him in a book. When compared with the book of Daniel, Ezekiel, and Isaiah, this book flows in unity, in harmony, and in agreement, leaving no doubt that Christ, the Light of the World, has chosen this seer to see into, *and past,* the church age, the salvation of Israel, the second coming of Christ, and into the millennial reign.

I am impressed in this chapter to emphasize the revealing of the prince of darkness–that age old spirit, working to defy the God of Heaven. In Revelation chapter 12, the Holy Spirit is revealing the past, declaring the future, as well as shining His light on the invisible spirit of darkness. The Prophet sees a great sign in Heaven: a woman clothed with the Sun, and the Moon under her feet, and upon her head a crown of twelve stars, and she was found with child. After travailing in birth to be delivered, there appeared a large red dragon and his tail drew one

OPPOSITE
"The Crowned Virgin,"
Gustave Dore

"St. John the Evangelist,"
Guido Remi

third of the stars of heaven. This dragon stood before the woman who was ready to be delivered, waiting to devour her child as soon as it was born. She brought forth a man child who was to rule the nations with a rod of iron and her child was caught up unto God and to His Throne. This magnificant, specific prophetic scene describes the nation of Israel as a woman clothed with the Sun, with the moon under her feet, and upon her head is a crown of twelve stars. This is Israel as a nation, the people of God, and heirs to the covenant of Abraham. For in Genesis chapter thirty-seven the prophet Joseph dreamed a dream. He saw the sun, the moon and the eleven stars bowing to him. He told this dream to his father, Jacob (or Israel). No doubt his mother would represent the moon, and the eleven brothers along with him would make up the twelve stars. Israel is often referred to as being married to God. The prophets foretold of the Messiah sitting on the throne of David. Isaiah clearly said, *"unto us a child is born...a son is given."*[1] It's clear that she gave birth to a man child–*"the seed of the woman shall come."* It is also clear that the dragon is revealed to be that old serpent called the devil, whose influence led one third of the angels of God to join him in his rebellion. Christ was saved from the demoniac Herod, during Herod's effort to kill the newborn king. By giving His life as the *"Lamb of God that takes away the sin of the world,"*[2] he paid for our sins, and rose again for our justification, and according to Scripture ascended up unto God and to His throne.[3] In this revelation we see the great enmity between the serpent and the people of God.

Israel is often spoken of as a woman married to God under the terms of the Law and the Prophets (Isa. 54:1-6, Jer. 3:1-14, Hos. 2:14-23). The Scriptures continue to show the malicious hatred and rebellious nature of this dragon by revealing what will take place in the second half of what we call the *time of Jacobs trouble,* the seven year tribulation period. With satanic resolve, he pursues Israel, in an attempt to destroy God's chosen ministers, who will be marked by God to stand against the antichrist, the false prophet, and the dragon. These Jewish champions have the mark of God placed upon them and represent 12,000 out of each of the 12 tribes of Israel, numbering 144,000.[4] Great persecution will be in the earth in those days when this bullying prince launches another battle to control, to consume the resources, and to oppose the purpose of God. It is at this time also that the Lord will send the two witnesses, Moses and Elijah. *"And I will give power unto my two witnesses,*

"The Archangel Michael," Guido Remi

and they shall prophesy a thousand two hundred and threescore days, clothed in sackcloth. These are the two olive trees, and the two candlesticks standing before the God of the earth. And if any man will hurt them, fire proceedeth out of their mouth, and devoureth their enemies: and if any man will hurt them, he must in this manner be killed" (Rev. 11:3-5). They will stand with Israel carrying supernatural power from on High during these forty-two months of tribulation.

As promised to the prophet Daniel, *"And at that time shall Michael stand up, the great prince which standeth for the children of thy people: and there shall be a time of trouble, such as never was since there was a nation even to that same time: and at that time thy people shall be delivered, every one that shall be found written in the book."[5] "And there was war in heaven: Michael and his angels fought against the dragon; and the dragon fought and his*

angels, And prevailed not; neither was their place found any more in heaven. And the great dragon was cast out, that old serpent, called the Devil, and Satan, which deceiveth the whole world: he was cast out into the earth, and his angels were cast out with him" (Rev. 12:7-9). This struggle between Michael and his angels is an actual war in heaven against the dragon and his angels. A battle between satan and God over the possession of the heavenlies; however, the dragon did not prevail and his place was found no more in heaven.

ISAIAH 14:12

"How hast thou fallen from heaven...O crusher of nations" (Rotherham).

"What a fall from heaven on high...How low and limp you lie" (Moffet).

"How you have fallen from heaven...sprawling helpless across the nations" (NEB).

"How are you fallen from heaven (O blasphemous, satanic King of Babylon)" (AMP).

This is a very clear performance of the *law of double-fulfillment*. During this time of defeat, satan and his armies are confined to the earth, knowing he has but a short time. He's ravaged with unholy wrath and anger. During these specifically defined most troublesome days–precisely numbered as 1,260 days or 42 months–the most ancient deception of the *titan religion* is revealed. A holy angel of God boldly proclaims, *Babylon is fallen! Babylon is fallen!* Her perversity and wrath are made known by the Lord (Rev. 14:8).

In the seventeenth chapter the Prophet is carried away by the Spirit, and sees a vision of a woman with the following words written on her forehead: MYSTERY, BABYLON, THE GREAT ,THE MOTHER OF HARLOTS AND ABOMINATIONS OF THE EARTH. She was

OPPOSITE
"The Distruction of Leviathan," Gustave Dore

ke thou that sleepest

Christ shall

sitting on a scarlet colored beast full of names of blasphemy, and arrayed in purple and scarlet. She was decked with gold and precious stones and pearls, and had a golden cup full of her abominations. She was drunk with the blood of the saints and with the blood of the martyrs of Jesus (Rev. 17 3-6).

This is the embodiment of the deception of the ages revealed in vision form. The age old deception of rebellion. This woman is the personification of the teaching of devils–the doctrines of perversion. She is acknowledged by scholars as a religious system; however, like a virus, the activities of her *mysteries* and *blasphemies* have worked to destroy morality, degenerate the fiber of societies, weaken the strength of nations, and deceive leaders of governments. This diabolical spiritual influence causes many nations to turn from God. When drunk with the wine of her deception, kings, nations and peoples cast off all restraint. The attire of this great harlot clearly identifies her as ideologically, philosophically, religiously, morally, and spiritually committed to seductions. She is satan's virus spreading his agenda. Through spiritism and fallacies invading the minds of political powers–eroding sensibilities, decaying commitments, severing loyalties and propelling the profane.

The purple, scarlet, precious stones, pearls, and the golden vessels she possesses are indicative of the wealth of the world. The chief bull of *Bashan, satan himself,* has utilized this destructive virus, endeavoring to control, steal , and possess the treasures of the earth. This deadly poison of ideology and false religion has transformed its presentation in order to appear harmless and rewarding to its targeted generation. MOTHER OF ABOMINATIONS OF THE EARTH was revealed to the wise as the image representing and embodying the age old message working to fertilize and foster a unity, tolerance, acceptance, and inclusion of all abominations, spiritual fornication, uncleanness, and paganism. This spiritual tool of the devil seeks to infiltrate every arena of society. The evident destructive nature, abilities of erosion, and mission to control, is hidden behind the shroud of a *harmless, intellectual, open-minded,* and *seemingly beneficial* facade.

As in the *Land of Bashan,* the immoral was termed *"Land of Romance"* under the rule of the mysterious *Astarte.* These deadly horns to gore are visible through the Word of God. This demonic agenda, packaged in an ancient invitation to the forbidden; this diabolical ideology that declares that nothing is off limits, disguised in reveling and celebration, drunk with the blood of the martyrs, enmity to the cause of the LORD AND HIS MESSIAH; this philosophical disguise masquerading as a desire for peace, has spread and contaminated over the years, by deceptively seeking *any common ground.* The goal of this bullying spirit, as in ancient Babylon, is *to rebel* against the truth while *claiming to stand for the truth.*

Hislop's *The Two Babylonians,* which quotes 260 sources, states that the ancient Babylonian cult started by *Nimrod* and his queen, *Semiramis,* spread among all nations. The objects of worship were the *Supreme Father,* the *Incarnate Female,* or *Queen of Heaven* and her *son.* This cult claimed the highest wisdom and the most divine secrets.[6] Since the dawn of time the devil has peddled *"wisdom"* to the ignorant–his nature, in a masque of *religiously correct hypocrisy.* His intention to build *"an invisible tower of Babel;"* his ambition to rule over the lives of men; and his agenda to facilitate a one-world government will be hindered or delayed through the goodness and power of God.

On April 28, 2008 the Lord gave me an open vision of a spirit that opposes Gods work on the planet. I heard the voice of the Lord say, "There is a spirit that wants to destroy ministry, break covenant, usurp authority, steal from My people, and keep My children trapped with the same patterns that he has used in generations past."

As a prophet of God, I believe that the times and the seasons in which we live, present the most accelerated opportunities for obedience. Yieldedness to the will of God, dedication to His cause, and mindfulness of His Holiness, cannot fail to yield the benefits of His promises. It is time to awaken unto His prophetic time. As a people who hold the truth of His Word to be the most *important beacon of light in our life, it is time for the covenant that we have to be the experience that we possess. It is time to allow God to lift us up through our humility; to prosper us through our charity; and to reward us through our dedication. Our faith, that overcomes the world system, cannot fail, for it works by love and love never fails. Because the love of God is in our hearts, we must choose to pursue the course of His Word and to obey the doctrine of His command. Our circumstances may seem as "giants," but our love for God is greater than our opposition. The challenges that oppose God's holy children are temporary. It is time for the believers to believe beyond their senses—seeing the invisible through promise; hearing the inaudible; accepting the unusual; serving wholeheartedly the Almighty God. It is time for God's spiritual house to determine to be spiritually holy—to allow the experience of the indwelling of Christ to have the highest place of expression in our life. For God's light shines in our heart. His Word is a lamp that will guide our direction at any dark time. God is light, and darkness can never overcome the light. I believe that God is raising up a spiritual people , disciplined by choice, determined to obey the word of God, and mindful of the necessity to trust in His ability—a victorious people willing to serve; to love with God's love; to give and receive; to pray, to study, and to stand. I believe that the church must rise and accept the commission to be the light of the world—shining with the light of Christ and shining for the cause of Christ.*

Through our study we have concluded that our world is shrouded with myth, lies, and unfounded belief systems. People are in the greatest position of need that we have ever seen. Unchangeable choices seem to be made *for us* and our society is transforming at a pace much too rapid to control. Forces which have been at work for thousands of years of recorded history are seeking their own agenda—spearheading wars, famine, and premeditated manipulations.

Information and propaganda is being impressed upon our societies, condoning and making repulsive lifestyles commonplace. Parents are increasingly removing their children from the school systems to protect them from gross inaccuracies concerning human behavior, rewritten histories, and ambiguous morality. Can we legislate morality while we know the undercurrent of these ancient Babylonian seductions are shrouded behind a guise of *acceptability?* Can we trust our leaders in the world to be sober and transparent, instead of incomprehensive and fleeting?

Our desire and commission is not to bring fear and intolerance, but to illuminate ideals and remind humanity that we must stand for what we believe. Our research has lead us to uncover the forbidden–*that which others would prefer to go unnoticed.* Our world, especially America, has arrived at the crossroads of *choice.* We must decide to be decisive, as a people, we are free moral agents with the inalienable right to choose action instead of passivity. The invisible war between light and darkness continues, the quality of our lives rest in our choices; however, *the fate of our enemy has already been written.* The victory of our Lord is already accomplished, and the choice to participate is now ours.

Special thanks to my beautiful wife, Robin, who worked tirelessly and kept on track in prayer, research, and writing, throughout the course of completing this historic text.

I love you,
Christian

SPECIAL MENTION

Co-Author & Executive Project Development —Dr. Robin Harfouche

Editorial, Research, & Development —Christie Harfouche

Art Direction and Archeological Research —John Harfouche

Graphic Design —Kevin Hamil & Robert Brady

Collaboration, Research, & Development —Esther Dan

Research & Discovery Confirmation —Christine Loretz

NOTES

CHAPTER 1
1. Sun Tzu, *The Art of War*.

CHAPTER 2
1. Genesis 3:14-15.
2. Isaiah 7:14.
3. James 2:19.
4. Isaiah 9:6.
5. See Matthew 16:19.
6. Isaiah 9:6.
7. See John 14:16-17.
8. John 1:1.

CHAPTER 3
1. Genesis 6:1-4.
2. See Genesis 6:4-6.
3. See Genesis 3:15.
4. Genesis 3:5.
5. Dr. Lester Sumrall, *The Battle of the Ages* (South Bend, IN: Sumrall Publishing, 1985).
6. *Dake Annotated Reference Bible*.
7. Daniel 3:24-25.
8. Flavius Josephus, *Antiquities of the Jews*.
9. Paul Pezron, *The Antiquities of Nations* (London, 1706).
10. Josephus, *Antiquities of the Jews*.
11. Ibid.
12. *Ante-Nicene Fathers* Vol. II, "A Plea for the Christians by Athenagoras of Athens," translated by Benjamin Plummer Pratten, Chapter XXIV.

13. *Ante-Nicene Fathers* Vol. I, "The Second Apology by Justin Martyr," translated by Philip Schaff et al., Chapter V.

14. *Ante-Nicene Fathers* Vol. VI, "From the Discourse on the Resurrection, Part III by Methodius," translated by Reverend Alexander Roberts.

15. James Strong, *Strong's Exhaustive Concordance of the Bible, NAS Exhaustive Concordance.*

16. Genesis 6:6-7.

17. Genesis 6:11-12.

18. Genesis 3:15.

19. See Genesis 6:12.

20. "The Complete Works of Flavius Josephus," Bible Study Tools Online, 2011, Chapter 3, http://www.biblestudytools.com/history/flavius-josephus/.

21. Ibid., Chapter 9.

Chapter 4

1. See 1 Timothy 4:1.

2. Genesis 6:3.

3. *Strong's Exhaustive Concordance, NAS Exhaustive Concordance*, Numbers 13 and Genesis 6:4, see also "Naphal."

4. *Strong's Exhaustive Concordance, NAS Exhaustive Concordance*, see also "Rapha."

5. Jude 1:14-15.

6. Pezron, *The Antiquities of Nations.*

7. Josephus, *Antiquities of the Jews.*

8. Pezron, *The Antiquities of Nations.*

9. Ibid.

10. Ibid.

11. Ibid.

12. Ibid.

13. Ibid.

14. Ibid.

15. Ibid.

16. Ibid.

17. Ibid.

18. Ibid.

Chapter 5

1. Genesis 5:22.

2. Hebrews 11:5.

3. *Dake,* commentary on "Ark." 94- 95

4. Ibid.

5. Ibid.

6. Ibid.

7. Dake Annotated Reference Bible.

8. Josephus, *Antiquities of the Jews,* Book I, Chapter 3.

9. See Luke 10:27.

Chapter 6

1. Josephus, *Antiquities of the Jews.*

2. Ibid.

3. Genesis 11:3-4.

4. *Dake Annotated Reference Bible.*

5. *Dake,* commentary on "Tower of Babel" 96. see also T*he Complete Works of Flavius Josephus,* Book 1, Chapter 4.

6. Dr. Christian Harfouche personal library, Vaulted.

7. *The Complete Works of Flavius Josephus, Antiquities of the Jews,* Book I.

8. Ibid.

9. Ibid.

10. Ibid.

11. Jeremiah 50:1-2.

12. Matthew 6:33.

13. Genesis 11:5-9.

14. Genesis 11:9.

15. Meillet and Cohen, *Languages of the World* (1952).

16. The term "Scripture" here refers to the scholarly study of the entirety of biblical Scripture.

17. Genesis 3:5.

Chapter 7

1. *The Complete Works of Flavius Josephus,* Book IV, Chapter 7.

2. Ibid.

3. Genesis 12:1-3.

4. Hebrews 11:10.

5. Book of Galatians; Hebrews 12:22.

6. Louis Ginzberg, *Legends of the Jews* qtd. in *Dake Annotated Reference Bible,* 1450, footnote k.

7. "The Song of the Three Holy Children" is a section in the Book of Daniel appearing in Roman Catholic and Eastern Orthodox Bibles.

8. Genesis 12:7-8.

9. Joshua 24:3.

10. Matthew 22:35-40.

11. Genesis 22:2; Jeremiah 31:6; Matthew 21:1; Mark 3:13; 2 Peter 1:18 and others.

12. Deuteronomy 9:9-10.

13. Josephus, *Antiquities of the Jews*

14. Matthew 4:8-11.

15. Matthew 5:1.

16. Josephus, Antiquities of the Jews.

17. Genesis 14:5.

18. *Dake Annotated Reference Bible.*

19. *Dake Annotated Reference Bible,* Genesis 14:13, Note d.

20. Josephus, Antiquities of the Jews.

21. Ibid.

22. Ibid.

23. Ibid.

24. Ibid.

25. Hebrews 7:2.

26. Exodus 32:13.

27. Galatians 3:29.

28. Genesis 25:11.

29. Genesis 32:24-28.

30. Genesis 32:24-28.

31. Genesis 32:30.

32. Genesis 32:30, Arabic Bible, synonyms "saved," "preserved," "rescued," "changed."

CHAPTER 8

1. Genesis 47:7.

2. *Dake,* Note H, Book of Exodus chapter 1, also Isaiah 52:4.

3. Exodus 1:8.

4. Isaiah 52:4.

5. Acts 7:17-18.

6. Acts 7:19-22.

7. Pezron, *The Antiquities of Nations.*

8. Josephus, *Antiquities of the Jews.*

9. Ibid.

10. Ibid.

11. Ibid.

12. Exodus 1:8.

13. *The Complete Works of Flavius Josephus,* Book II, Chapter 9; Dake, footnote t, Exodus 1:15

14. Josephus, *Antiquities of the Jews.*

15. Exodus 1:11.

16. Exodus 1:11.

17. Exodus 1:15-17.

18. Josephus, *Antiquities of the Jews.*

19. Ibid.

20. Acts 7:20.

21. Josephus, *Antiquities of the Jews.*

22. Ibid.

23. *The Complete Works of Flavius Josephus,* Book II, Chapter 9.

24. Acts 7:22.

25. Josephus, *Antiquities of the Jews.*

26. Ibid.

27. Acts 7:22.

28. See Exodus 2:14.

29. Exodus 2:14.

30. Exodus 3:1; Exodus 2:21.

31. Josephus, *Antiquities of the Jews.*

32. Exodus 3:2.

33. Josephus, *Antiquities of the Jews.*

34. Hebrews 1:7.

35. Exodus 3:5-7.

36. Josephus, *Antiquities of the Jews.*

37. *Dake Annotated Reference Bible.*

38. Exodus 3:14-15.

39. *Dake Annotated Reference Bible,* Exodus 3:14, Note d.

40. Exodus 3:20.

41. Exodus 3:22.

42. *Dake Annotated Reference Bible,* Exodus 3:22, Note r; *Strong's Exhaustive Concordance, NAS Exhaustive Concordance.*

43. Josephus, *Antiquities of the Jews.*

44. Ibid.

45. Exodus 12:33.

46. Exodus 1:8-12; Isaiah 52:4; Acts 7:17-22.

47. 1 Samuel 1:17,20; 8:10; Psalm 2:8. The Hebrew word *Sha'al* is better translated "demand" or "require" as it was in 173 other occurrences in the Bible. The word is inaccurately translated "borrow" only six times.

48. Hebrews 11:28-29.

49. Hebrews 11:29.

50. Exodus 15:2-3.

51. Josephus, *Antiquities of the Jews.*

52. Ibid.

53. Ibid.

54. Exodus 24:12.

55. Exodus 24:10.

CHAPTER 9

1. Exodus 24:17-18.

2. Exodus 32:7.

3. Exodus 32:2-3.

4. Exodus 32:8.

5. Exodus 32:5.

6. Exodus 32:6.

7. 1 Samuel 15:23.

8. Pezron, *The Antiquities of Nations.*

9. Exodus 32:7.

10. Exodus 32:17-20.

11. Exodus 32:21-28.

12. Deuteronomy 8:18.

13. Mark 3:24.

14. Josephus, *Antiquities of the Jews.*

CHAPTER 10

1. Acts 7:37-43.

2. Amos 5:26.

3. Amos 5:27.

4. Jude 1:13.

5. Carolina Martinez, "Cassini Images Bizarre Hexagon on Saturn," NASA, March 27, 2007, accessed December 22, 2010, http://www.nasa.gov/mission_pages/cassini/media/cassini-20070327.html.

6. Deuteronomy 32:17.

7. Leviticus 17:7.

8. Galatians 5:19-21.

9. Josephus, *Antiquities of the Jews.*

10. *Dake Annotated Reference Bible.*

11. Numbers 14:2-3.

12. Numbers 14:20-21.

13. Josephus, *Antiquities of the Jews.*

14. Hebrews 3:19.

15. Josephus, *Antiquities of the Jews.*

CHAPTER 11

1. Daniel 1:5.

2. Daniel 1:6-7.

3. *Smith's Bible Dictionary,* "Shinar" (country of two rivers); *Thompson Chain-reference Bible* archeological supplement, 1749; *The Complete Works of Flavius Josephus* on Abraham Book I, Chapter 7; Pezron, *The Antiquities of Nations.*

4. *NAS Exhaustive Concordance; Dake Annotated Reference Bible,* Notes on Daniel, "Names Defined."

5. Daniel 2:1-18.

6. Daniel 2:30-35.

7. Daniel 2:37.

8. Daniel 2:38.

9. See Daniel 2:39-43.

10. Daniel 2:44.

11. Daniel 2:47-48.

12. Megasthenes was a Greek historian and diplomat (c. 350-282 B.C.).

13. *The Complete Works of Flavius Josephus,* Book X, Chapter 11.

14. Ibid.

15. Ephesians 6:12.

16. Ephesians 6:12.

17. Daniel 3:12.

18. Deuteronomy 5:6-9.

19. *Dake Annotated Reference Bible,* Exodus 20:4, Note o; *Strong's Exhaustive Concordance; NAS Exhaustive Concordance.*

20. Daniel 3:24-25.

21. Daniel 3:29-30.

22. Josephus, *Antiquities of the Jews.*

23. Daniel 4:6-9.

24. *Dake Annotated Reference Bible.*

25. Daniel 4:13-17.

26. Daniel 4:24-25.

27. Josephus, *Antiquities of the Jews.*

28. Daniel 4:30.

29. Daniel 4:31-32.

30. Daniel 4:34-35.

CHAPTER 12

1. *Thompson Chain Reference Bible,* Archeological supplement, 4374 ERECH.

2. Ibid.

3. Ibid., Genesis 10:10.

4. *Thompson Chain Reference Bible,* Archeological supplement, 4418.

5. Ibid.

6. Pezron, *The Antiquities of Nations.*

7. Ibid.

8. Ibid.

9. Ibid.

10. Josephus, *Antiquities of the Jews.*

CHAPTER 13

1. Josephus, *Antiquities of the Jews.*

2. Ibid.

3. Isaiah 14, *Word 26 Translations, The Peshita Aramaic Translation, Wycliffe Translation, Tyndale Translation.*

4. Ibid.

5. *Catholic Encyclopedia,* Isaiah 14; *Peshita Aramaic Translation.*

CHAPTER 14

1. See Psalms 22:12; *Dake Annotated Reference Bible,* Note on Verse 12

2. 1 Kings 4:13; Deuteronomy 3:1-8; *Dake Annotated Reference Bible,* 401, "The Argob;" 337, Note g; Joshua 12:4,5; See Bible maps; Personal Library Dr. Christian Harfouche, Vaulted.

3. Author's personal experience and travels

4. *Dake Annotated Reference Bible,* 90- 91 (proofs giants were sons of angels); Deuteronomy 3:10-11 KJV; Joshua 12:4-5.

5. Psalm 22:7-8.

6. Psalm 22:22-26.

7. *Smith's Bible Dictionary,* "Boundaries Defined: Bashan"; Personal Library Dr. Christian Harfouche, Vaulted.

8. Mark 9:2.

9. Mark 5:9.

10. Joshua 1:6,9.

11. 1 Samuel 17:4-6; 2 Samuel 21:16,22; 1 Chronicles 20:4-8; *The Complete Works of Flavius Josephus,* Book VII, Chapter 12.

12. Romans 8:34.

13. 1 Corinthians 2:8 KJV.

CHAPTER 15

1. Isaiah 9:6.

2. John 1:29.

3. John 20:17.

4. Revelation 14:1.

5. Daniel 12:1.

6. Alexander Hislop, "The Two Babylons," Biblebelievers.com, accessed December 22, 2010, http://www.biblebelievers.com/babylon/.

BIBLE REFERENCE MATERIAL

TGB   *The Geneva Bible* A.D. 1560

TTM   *The Thomas Matthews* A.D. 1549

TBFE   *The Bishop's First Edition* A.D. 1568

KJ   *The King James Subscriber's Edition* A.D. 1611

        Harmony of the Gospels A.D. 1947

        John Foxe Ecclesiastical History: Vol I, II, III A.D. 1684

        Peshitta Aramaic Bible Text

AAT   *The Bible: An American Translation*

ASV   *The American Standard Version* (Star Bible & Tract)

ABPS   *The Bible* (American Baptist Publication Society) (Cornell
            University Library)

AMP   *The Amplified Bible* (Zondervan Publishing)

BAS   *The Bible in Basic English* (Cambridge University Press)

JERUS *The Jerusalem Bible* (DOUBLEDAY & CO INC)

KNOX   A translation from the Latin Vulgate in the Light of the
            Hebrew and Greek

        Originals (Sheed & Ward)

LAM   *The Bible from Ancient Eastern Manuscripts* (Harper Collins
            Publishers)

TOR   *The Torah: The Five Books of Moses* (Henry Holt and Co.)

TAY   *The Living Bible* (Tyndale Publishers)

RV   *The Revised Version* (Ignatius Press)

RSV   *Revised Standard Version* (Plume)

RHM   *The Emphasized Bible* (The Standard Publishing Company)

SEPT   *The Septuagint* (The Falcon's Wing Press)

SPRL   *A Translation of the Old Testament Scriptures from the Original
            Hebrew* (James Nisbet and Co, 1885)

ABUV   *American Bible Union Version* (American Bible Union, 1868)

TCNT   *Twentieth Century New Testament* (Cornell University Library)

RIEU   *The Four Gospels* (United Bible Societies)

BA   *Bible Archaeology* (Baker Books)

NIV   *New International Version: Arabic/English* (Zondervan)

SEC   *Strong's Exhaustive Concordance* (Thomas Nelson)

HBD   *Holman Bible Dictionary* (Broadman & Holman Publishers)

TBOTA   *The Battle of the Ages* (Sumrall Publishing A.D. 1985)

SBD   *Smith's Bible Dictionary* (Hendrickson Publishers, A.D. 1962)

TCOEM   *The Church of England Magazine* (Tate Publishing)

TME   *The Modern Encyclopedia* (The Algamated Press, A.D. 937)

TCOS   *Nelson's New Illustrated Bible Dictionary* (Oxford Bible, A.D. 1868)

ASB   *Archaeological Study Bible* (Zondervan Publishing)

The Holy Bible Arabic (The Bible Society)

Word Studies in the Greek New Testament Vol 3 (Wm. B Eerdmans Publishing Co. 1961)

World History in Its Geographic Setting (Chicago Publishing, 1961)

Zondervan Expanded Concordance (Zondervan Publishing, 1968)

A Theological Work Book of the Bible (Alan Richardson D.D. S.C.M. Press, A.D. 1950)

Dake's Annotated Reference Bible (Dake Publishing)

The Thompson Chain Reference Bible (B.B. Kirkbride Bible Company)

AMG   *The Complete Word Study New Testament* (AMG Publishers)

Porter, T.L *The Giant Cities of Bashan* (Thomas Nelson, A.D. 1864)

Kenneth S. Wuest (Wm. B Eerdmans Publishing Co. 1961)

ANCIENT HISTORICAL SOURCES

The Histories–Herodotus

The Antiquities of Nations, Pezron (1706)

The Complete Works of Josephus, Flavius Josephus

Eustathius Ofantioch, Bishop of Antioch (A.D. 320)

St. Isodore of Seville (Last Scholar of the Ancient World)

Apologies for Primitive Christians

History of the Jews, Malchus Cleodemus (2nd Century B.C.)

The Targum of Jonathan

Earliest Witness of the Canonical Character of All the Four Gospels, St. Irenaeus (A.D. 202)

Strabo Geography Book XIV

Fourth Book Accounts of India, Megasthenes (288 B.C.)

Hexameron (A.D. 370)

Septuagint

St. Jerome

Stephen of Bizantium

Pessidonius (135 B.C. – 51 B.C.)

Diodorus Siculus (1st Century B.C.)

Plutarch (A.D. 46 – A.D. 120)

Friend of St. Augustine, St. Possidonius (A.D. 379)

Sanchoniathon Antiquity of Phoenicia (1300 B.C.)

Bishop Eusebius (A.D. 263 – A.D. 339)

Phornutus

Simias of Rhodes (3rd to 2nd B.C.)

Hesychius The Grammarian (5th Century)

Diodorus Siculus (1st Century B.C.)

Tertullian (A.D. 160 – A.D. 220)

Philocorus The Historian (261 B.C.)

Athenagoras (A.D. 133 – A.D. 190)

Theophilus of Antioch (A.D. 412)

Minutius Felix (A.D. 170)

Arnobius (A.D. 330)

St. Augustine (A.D. 354 – A.D. 426)
Lactantius (A.D. 240 – A.D. 320)
Cicero (A.D. 106 – A.D. 43)
Suidas
Chronicle of Alexandria
St. Cyril of Alexandria (A.D. 376 – A.D. 444)
Talmud
Targum
Hecataeus of Miletus (550 B.C. – 476 B.C.)

PHOTOGRAPHY CREDITS

King Sargon's Lammasu Page 1 Opposite: *Trjames, Wikimedia Commons. Creative Commons Attribution ShareAlike 3.0*

Minoan Bull Head Page 3: *Wolfgang Sauber. Creative Commons Attribution-Share Alike 3.0 Unported*

Limestone bull capital Page 5: *Vassil, Wikimedia Commons. Public Domain*

Adam and Eve are driven out of eden, Page 6: *Gustave Dore. Public Domian*

"Sturz der Rebellischen Engel", Page 9: *Sebastiano Ricci, 1720. Public Domain*

Abu Simbel Temple, Page 10: *Hedwig Storch, Wikimedia Commons. Creative Commons Attribution Unported 2.0*

Xerxes I relief, Page 11: *Ginolerhino, Wikimedia Commons. Creative Commons Attribution ShareAlike 3.0*

Tachara Palace Relief, Page 14: *Hansueli Krapf, Wikimedia Commons. Creative Commons Attribution ShareAlike 3.0*

Gilgamesh with Lion, Page 16: *Public Domain*

Page from the Codex Gigas, Page 19: *Kungliga biblioteket. Public Domain*

Narmer Palette, Page 20-21: *Public Domain*

Sling, Page 24: *Neal Grout. Public Domain*

"David und Goliath", Page 25: *Osmar Schindler. Public Domain*

"Slaying Goliath", Page 26: *Peter Paul Rubens. Public Domain*

"David and Goliath", Page 29: *Gustave Dore. Public Domain*

Standing Stone, Page 30: *Used under License. All Rights Reserved iStockphoto*

Female Figure, Page 32: *egotechnique, Wikimedia Commons. Creative Commons Attribution 2.5 Generic*

3 neolithic bull representations, Page 33: *ChristianChirita, Wikimedia Commons. Creative Commons Attribution-Share Alike 3.0 Unported*

Temple of Bel full, Page 35: *Yvonnefm, Wikimedia Commons. Creative Commons Attribution-Share Alike 3.0 Unported*

2 Images of the Temple of Bel, Page 36-37: *Zeledi, Wikimedia Commons. Creative Commons Attribution ShareAlike 3.0*

Carnac, Page 38: *GFDL, Wikimedia Commons. Creative Commons Attribution ShareAlike 3.0*

Stonehenge Trilithon, Page 39: *Ciukes, Flickr. Creative Commons Attribution Generic 2.0*

Stonehenge sun, Pages 40 and 41: *Simon Wakefield. Creative Commons Attribution 2.0 Generic*

Giant Builds Stonehenge, Page 43: *Roman de Brut manuscript, British Library. Public Domain*

"The Deluge," Pages 44 and 45: *Engraving by William Miller after John Martin, Public Domain*

"The Egyptians Drown in the Sea," Page 46: *Gustave Dore. Public Domain*

The Deluge, Page 48: *Painting by Francis Danby, Tate Gallery, London. Public Domain*

God helps Noah build, Page 51: *Julius Schnorr von Carolsfeld, Public Domain*

Noah receives Dove with olive branch, Page 52: *Andrei Ryabushkin, Public Domain*

Guardian angel, Page 54: *Public Domain*

"The Dove Sent Forth from the Ark," Page 55: *Gustave Dore, Public Domain*

The Tower of Babel, Page 56: *Pieter Bruegel de Oude. Public Domain*

King Sargon Bronze Head, Page 58: *Iraqi Directorate General of Antiquities. Public Domain*

Relief from Nineveh, Page 59: *Marie-Lan Nguyen, Wikimedia Commons. Creative Commons Attribution 2.5 Generic*

Assyrian relief of Winged Being, Page 60: *Rosemania, Wikimedia Commons. Creative Commons 2.0 Generic*

Winged Man-Headed Lion, Page 61: *Lusitana, Wikimedia Commons. Creative Commons Attribution 2.5 Generic*

Tchongha Zanbil Ziggurat, Pages 62-63: *dynamosquito, Flickr. Creative Commons Attribution-Share Alike 2.0 Generic*

Ashurbanipal hunting relief, Nineveh, Page 64: *Emmanuel Muller-Baden. Public Domain*

Destruction of Susa, Page 65: *Zereshk, Wikipedia. Creative Commons ShareAlike 3.0*

Symbol of Ashur, Page 66: *Public Domain*

Faravahar at sunset, Page 67: *Roodiparse, Wikimedia Commons. Public Domain*

Lamentation Over the Death of the First-Born In Egypt, Page 105: *Charles Sprague Pearce. Public Domain*

Delivery of Israel out of Egypt, Pages 108-109: *Samuel Colman 1830, Public Domain.*

Weapons of Queen Ahhotep, Page 111: *"History of Egypt, Chaldea, Syria, Babylonia, and Assyria", General Books. Public Domain*

Golden Apis Head, Back Inside Flap of Dustcover, and Page 112: *Gryffindor, Wikimedia Commons. Creative Commons Attribution ShareAlike 3.0*

"The Adoration of the Golden Calf," Page 115: *Nicolas Poussin 1633-4. Public Domain*

Apis Stele, Page 116: *Loic Evanno, Wikimedia Commons. Creative Commons Attribution ShareAlike 3.0*

Four Horned Khnum, Page 117: *Jon Bodsworth. Public Domain*

Dendera Relief, Page 118: *Bernard Gagnon, Wikimedia Commons. Creative Commons Attribution-Share Alike 3.0 Unported*

Mycaenen Bull Rhyton with Flower, Page 119: *Sailko, Wiikimedia commons. Creative Commons Attribution ShareAlike 3.0*

"Moses Breaking the Tablets of the Law," Page 121: *Gustave Dore. Public Domain*

"Elijah," Page 123: *Jose de Ribera. Public Domain*

"Elijah Resuscitating the Son of the Widow of Zarephath," Page 127: *Louis Hersent. Public Domain*

"Slaughter of the Prophets of Baal," Page 128: *Gustave Dore. Public Domain*

"The Victory of Joshua Over the Amalekites," Page 130: *Nicolas Poussin 1625-6. Public Domain*

Mt. Sinai, Page 132: *Florian Prischl, Wikimedia Commons. Creative Commons Attribution-Share Alike 3.0 Unported*

Molech, Page 133: *Public Domain*

Saturn Pole Photos, Page 134: *NASA. Public Domain*

Stele of King Melishipak, Page 136: *Marie-Lan Nguyen, Wikimedia Commons. Public Domain*

Baal With Thunderbolt, Page 137: *Marie-Lan Nguyen, Wikimedia Commons. Public Domain*

Hittite Cup, Page 138: *Homonihilis, Wikimedia Commons. Public Domain*

Emblem of Ankara, Page 140: *Bjorn Christian Torrison, Wikimedia Commons. Creative Commons Attribution-Share Alike 3.0 Unported*

Clay Hittite Rhyton, Page 140: *Homonihilis, Wikimedia Commons. Public Domain*

Bronze Hittite Rhyton, Page 141: *Mark Randall Dawson. Creative Commons*

Razor, Page 179: *Nasko, Wikimedia Commons. Public Domain*

Alexander the Coin, Page 180: *CNG Coins (http://www.cngcoins.com). Creative Commons Attribution ShareAlike 3.0*

"Alexander the Great in the Temple of Jerusalem," Page 181: *Sebastiano Conca. Public Domain*

Isaiah 14:9-18, Page 182: *Copyright Christian Harfouche Ministries all rights reserved.*

Hanging Gardens, Page 184: *Martin Heeskerck, Public Domain*

Kudurru, Page 185: *Rama, Wikimedia Commons. Creative Commons Attribution-Share Alike 2.0 France*

Star, Moon, Sun, Page 186: *See Page 146*

Closeup of Kudurru, Page 187: *Rama, Wikimedia Commons Attribution-Share Alike 2.0 France*

"The Prophet Isaiah," Page 188: *Raffaello Sanzio, 1511-1512. Public Domain*

"St. Jerome in His Study," Page 190: *Domenico Ghirlandaio. Public Domain*

"Saint Jerome," Page 191: *Michelangelo Merisi da Caravaggio. Public Domain*

Kursi Ruin, Page 192: *Copyright iStockphoto. All rights reserved. Used under license.*

Blessing Goddess, Page 194: *Marie-Lan Nguyen. Creative Commons Attribution 2.5 Generic*

Obelisk temple, Page 195: *Heretiq, Wikimedia Commons, Creative Commons Attribution-Share Alike 2.5 Generic*

Bull Rhyton, Page 197: *Marie-Lan Nguyen, Wikimedia Commons, Public Domain*

Gilgal Refa'im, Page 198: *Wikimedia Commons, Creative Commons Attribution ShareAlike 3.0*

Makthar Megalith, Page 200: *Pradigue, Wikimedia Commons. Creative Commons Attribution 3.0 Unported*

Lanyon quoit, Page 201: *waterborough, Wikimedia Commons. Public Domain*

House of a Giant, Page 202: *"The Giant Cities of Bashan and Syria's Holy Places" J.L. Porter D.D. 1877. Public Domain*

Ruins in Bashan, Page 203: *"The Giant Cities of Bashan and Syria's Holy Places" J.L. Porter D.D. 1877. Public Domain*

"The Crown Virgin," Page 204: *Gustave Dore. Public Domain*

"St. John the Evangelist," Page 206: *Guido Reni. Public Domain*

"Archangel Michael Tramples Satan," Page 207: *Guido Reni. Public Domain*

"The Destruction of Leviathan," Page 208: *Gustave Dore. Public Domain*

"Angel of Resurrection," Page 210-211: *Forever Wiser, Flikr. Creative Commons Attribution 2.5 Generic*

The eastern entrance to the John Adams building, Library of Congress, United States. Sculpted on these bronze doors are the images of gods from ancient civilizations from all over the world.
Carol M. Highsmith, Public Domain

Nimrod's fortress, a fortress named after Nimrod, located in the Land of Bashan.
David King, Creative Commons Attribution 2.0 Generic

"It is entirely possible that the pyramids of Egypt, the giant cities of Bashan, and other huge monuments of construction, will remain an unsolved mystery, unless they are accepted as the result of the labor and the skill of angels." —Dr. Christian Harfouche

In the right hands, This Book will Change Lives!

Most of the people who need this message will not be looking for this book. To change their lives, you need to put a copy of this book in their hands.

> *But others (seeds) fell into good ground, and brought forth fruit, some a hundred-fold, some sixty-fold, some thirty-fold* (Matthew 13:8).

Our ministry is constantly seeking methods to find the good ground, the people who need this anointed message to change their lives. Will you help us reach these people?

> *Remember this—a farmer who plants only a few seeds will get a small crop. But the one who plants generously will get a generous crop* (2 Corinthians 9:6).

EXTEND THIS MINISTRY BY SOWING
3 BOOKS, 5 BOOKS, 10 BOOKS, **OR MORE TODAY,**
AND BECOME A LIFE CHANGER!

Thank you,

Don Nori Sr., Publisher
Destiny Image
Since 1982

DESTINY IMAGE PUBLISHERS, INC.

*"Speaking to the Purposes of God for This Generation
and for the Generations to Come."*

VISIT OUR NEW SITE HOME AT
WWW.DESTINYIMAGE.COM

FREE SUBSCRIPTION TO DI NEWSLETTER

Receive free unpublished articles by top DI authors, exclusive

discounts, and free downloads from our best and newest books.

Visit www.destinyimage.com to subscribe.

Write to: Destiny Image
             P.O. Box 310
             Shippensburg, PA 17257-0310

Call: 1-800-722-6774

Email: orders@destinyimage.com

For a complete list of our titles or to place an order
online, visit www.destinyimage.com.

FIND US ON FACEBOOK OR FOLLOW US ON TWITTER.

www.facebook.com/destinyimage   facebook

www.twitter.com/destinyimage   twitter